Diablo –
Trouble at Mercy Ranch

Gabi Adam

Diablo –
Trouble at Mercy Ranch

Cover photo: © Bob Langrish
Cover layout: Stabenfeldt A/S
Translated by Barclay House Publishing
Typeset by Roberta L. Melzl
Editor: Bobbie Chase
Printed in Germany, 2009

ISBN: 978-1-934983-04-1

Stabenfeldt, Inc.
457 North Main Street
Danbury, CT 06811
www.pony4kids.com

Available exclusively through PONY.

A person is often different than he seems.
So, always look twice to really see him.

Chapter 1

Logan Bendix was one of those boys who made Ricki Sulai's hair stand on end right from the beginning, even at a distance.

"A pretty face with nothing else behind it," was her first comment after she had given her new classmate the once-over.

However, her friends Cathy Sutherland and Beth Pendleton were smitten.

"Did you girls get a look at that new guy, Logan? Wow, is he ever gorgeous!" Beth raved, as she and her pals stood near the high school bike stands, where they always met after class.

"Exactly my point!" responded Ricki. "He's *too* good looking, and he knows it! You guys saw how he acted in class on his very first day. He thinks he's so great just because he's good looking and comes from New York City. Well I don't like the way he acts! He's arrogant and stuck up and he thinks we're hicks from the sticks!"

"Oh, I don't think so. After all, everyone is a little weird the first day in a new school and a new town, don't you think?" Cathy was obviously on Logan's side, too, and her girlfriend frowned at her, annoyed.

"I can see I'm not going to change either of your opinions of him. I don't know why you like him. He hasn't even said hello to us, even though he sits right next to us." Ricki clamped her backpack onto her bike rack and buckled the straps to hold it in place.

"But he rides and has his own horse," interrupted Kevin Thomas, Ricki's boyfriend, who overheard the girls' conversation while walking over to meet them. "That gives him a *few* points, doesn't it?"

Ricki hesitated.

"He has his own horse? How do you know?"

Kevin grinned broadly.

"I'm not going to reveal my source," he teased. "Actually, I just overheard Logan on his cell phone."

"Hmmm." Pensively, Ricki got on her bike. "Just because he rides doesn't make him a nice guy."

"Ricki, stop it! You don't know Logan yet, so you shouldn't judge him so quickly." Sixteen-year-old Lillian Bates, who had up to that point just been listening to her younger friends, shook her head with displeasure.

"Now you're defending him, too. You haven't even seen him yet," grumbled Ricki.

"That doesn't make any difference. You can't condemn someone just because he seems standoffish on his first day of school. After all, he doesn't know anyone, and you guys didn't even make an effort to introduce yourselves to him."

"That's true," agreed Cathy, and Ricki realized that she

was alone today in her opinion, even though the friends usually agreed on everything.

"Think what you want. Someday you'll see that I'm right!" Ricki said angrily.

"Or not," laughed Kevin, giving his girlfriend a kiss on her cheek. "Actually, you shouldn't even be thinking about the guy, because you have me! I don't know why you're so worked up about this."

"I'm not!"

"Okay, then," Lillian grinned at her, amused. "So, what about going home now? I have an incredible amount of homework today, and if I don't at least start on it soon, I can forget about going riding this afternoon. Holli will be totally freaked if he's the only one who gets left behind in his stall, while you and your horses go riding."

"You're right, it's time to get going. Can we meet at Ricki's about three o'clock?" asked Cathy as she looked around at the others.

"Three o'clock is okay for me," answered Kevin.

"Then I'll meet you all at Echo Lake around four, if that's okay," added Beth, who boarded her horse at Carlotta Mancini's Mercy Ranch instead of in the Sulais' stable. Echo Lake lay approximately in the middle, between the two properties.

"Okay, see you later," the friends said good-bye to each other before riding off in different directions. Only Ricki and Lillian went the same way, because they lived within sight of each other's homes.

"Hey, did something bad happen to you today? You seem like you're in such a sore mood," said Lillian. Without saying much more, the two girls rode home.

"Ohhh, my head is spinning! I don't think I've ever had to learn so many vocabulary words all at once," groaned Lillian, as she, Cathy, Kevin, and Ricki, made their way across the yard from the Sulais' house to the stable, where their horses were stabled. "French and then Spanish ... I'm going to go crazy!"

Kevin laughed. "Holli will shake you up in the saddle, and that should fix your brain again."

"Let's hope so," grinned Lillian, as Cathy opened the stable door. Their horses were already whinnying a greeting, as if they knew it was about time for their ride.

As always, Ricki's eyes began to shine when she saw her black horse, Diablo.

"Hello, my sweetie. Did you miss me?" Ricki said, as she did every time she entered the stable. She walked over to his stall and put her arms around the gelding's huge head. She closed her eyes in complete happiness and breathed in the smell of his coat, while the others greeted their horses enthusiastically.

Kevin gave his roan, Sharazan, an enormous carrot, and Cathy stroked the forehead of the dun, Rashid. She felt very lucky that Carlotta had lent her the horse to take care of and allowed her free rein with him, as though he belonged to her. From time to time, when Carlotta came to visit Ricki's mother, Brigitte, she also visited her long-maned gelding out in the Sulais' stable. She also saw him often when the kids rode out to Mercy Ranch, her home for retired and unwanted horses.

Lillian patted her white horse, Doc Holliday, on his neck

affectionately and greeted Chico, the little donkey that belonged to the Bates family. He shared the fifth stall with Carlotta's pony mare, Salina.

"Salina has shaped up really nicely, don't you think?" asked Lillian.

Ricki stepped over to her friend and nodded enthusiastically.

"That's for sure. When I think of how thin she was when I found her ..." For a moment, in her mind, she saw the abandoned farm she had discovered one day, and the starving Salina, who had been all skin and bones then. The memory made Ricki sigh aloud, but then a smile spread across her face.

"I think it's awesome and fitting that Carlotta made Mercy Ranch out of Salina's old home. It's such a great place, and it has the best stable in the whole area!"

"What about your own stable? Or is that no big deal?" teased Kevin, as he began to brush Sharazan's coat until it shone.

"Oh, Kev, you know what I mean. Our stable is great, but Mercy Ranch is just ... different." Ricki opened the gate of Diablo's stall and led her horse out into the corridor, while she thought about how great it would be if there were a few extra stalls in the stable so that they, too, could give old or mistreated horses a new home.

"Say, Kevin, earlier today you said that the new kid has his own horse," Cathy suddenly remembered as she led Rashid, who was already saddled, out of his stall.

"Which new kid?" asked Kevin, having put the after-school discussion out of his mind.

"Logan!"

"Oh, you mean *that* guy."

"Do you know what kind of horse it is and where he boards it?" Cathy probed further.

"Hey, I have no idea. *You* sit right next to him. Ask him yourself tomorrow!" Kevin looked at his friends. "Aren't you guys ready yet? Can we get going?"

"Just a minute, I still have to buckle the snaffle ... Okay, now I'm ready," said Lillian and she led Doc Holliday out of his stall.

"Where are we riding? If we go straight to Echo Lake we'll get there too early. Beth won't be there until around four o'clock."

Together, the kids led the horses outside into the yard.

"Maybe we could –" Kevin began, but at that moment he was interrupted by Jake Alcott, the elderly groom who looked after the Sulais' stable and its residents, and was like a grandfather to Ricki and her younger brother, Harry.

"Ricki! Ricki! Wait!" Jake, whom Ricki had to thank for her horse, came walking over to the kids from his cottage, as fast as he could. Lupo, his old tomcat, sprang up behind him and fled under Diablo when he spied Rosie, Ricki's dog, dozing in the sun.

"Can you ride past the mill and order a few sacks of oats and bran? Oh, yeah, and we'll need mineral feed soon, too. Tell Kubitsch to deliver everything tomorrow morning."

Kevin grinned.

"Thanks, Jake. You're a real treasure!"

"Huh?" The old man frowned, perplexed.

"Well, now we don't have to decide where to ride."

"Oh!" Now Jake understood. A little awkwardly, he bent

10

down and picked up Lupo, still hiding under Diablo's belly, just to be sure he wouldn't get stepped on when the kids swung up into their saddles.

"Don't go too far today," the old man warned them, his head bent back as he stared at the sky. "It's very muggy. I get the feeling we're in for a thunderstorm."

"Do you really think so? There's not a cloud in the sky," Ricki said, looking at the groom in surprise.

"I feel it in my bones," claimed Jake, and then he headed to the stable.

"Jake has stormy bones," smiled Kevin, then steered Sharazan onto the small trail that led through the field, directly toward the mill.

"Don't laugh, Kevin. Jake's predictions are almost always right. But, not to change the subject ... I suggest we go to Carlotta's first, to get Beth, and then ride to the mill," said Ricki, and she rode Diablo to the front of the little group of riders. "If we ride to the mill first, we'll never get to Echo Lake by four."

* * *

Logan was on his way to the riding stable where his parents had rented a stall for his horse. Star wouldn't be there long, however, because the Bendix family's new property had a small stable that needed just a little renovation, and then it would be the new home for Logan's horse.

While the boy walked quickly down the road, he thought about the past few months and about his friends in New York.

Friends? he thought and frowned deeply. Were they really "friends," with whom he had spent most of his free time and, for the most part, whose fault it was that he had landed here in this hick town?

11

Why was I stupid enough to get involved in those idiotic games? he asked himself for the hundredth time. The police had come to his parents' door with various complaints of property damage – and not just once – because he had let himself be persuaded to spray-paint dumb slogans and words on buildings, walls, and, one time, even on a car. Well, anyway, it had been a real mess when his father's boss caught him in the act and made a big deal of it. Logan's parents were ashamed of their son and embarrassed for their family, so they decided to leave the city after all that had happened. They hoped with all their hearts that the decision to move would take Logan away from the bad influence of his so-called friends.

The boy sighed. He missed New York and all the stuff there was to do there. On the other hand, he now regretted the bad things he had done, and was grateful that his parents had decided not to sell his beloved Star as punishment for his behavior. He still couldn't explain to himself why he had done what he did.

Enough of that! He shook his head to drive away the images of the past, and he directed his thoughts to Star. He couldn't wait to see him.

When Logan entered the riding stable and breathed in the enticing smell of the horses, he glanced at his watch before rushing down the corridor. Star would have been here for about an hour and a half, if the employee at the horse transport company had kept his word.

If Mom hadn't made me do that stupid homework first, I could have been here when Star arrived! The building complex was huge, with stalls of various sizes both inside and out, and he had no idea which stall Star was in.

As Logan ran past the light, pleasant stalls, he sensed the other horse owners looking at him as he passed. They reminded him of his first day at his new school that morning.

"Hi!" said Logan, very friendly, but inwardly defensive. There was nothing he hated more than people staring at him. Why did he always have the feeling that they knew about his failures in The Big Apple and were judging him?

Glancing all around him, he stopped walking.

"Hello, young man. You seem to be looking for something. May I help you?" one of the riders asked.

Logan, who had, of course, heard the man's voice clearly, just rolled his eyes and acted as if he didn't realize he was being spoken to.

I've got to get out of here! he thought in a panic, and hurried away.

If only he knew where Star was. Maybe he should have asked that rider and not just run away.

Suddenly he slapped his palm against his forehead.

"Oh, I'm such an idiot," Logan mumbled to himself. "Why am I walking through the inside of the stable, when I know that Mom rented an outside stall for Star?"

Quickly, the boy ran toward a narrow emergency exit, which led outside.

Logan sighed with relief when he was back in the fresh air. Everything had seemed so closed in, but that was because everyone he passed looked strangely at him.

Nevertheless, this stable was phenomenal; he had to admit that. Everything was completely modern, and Logan guessed the riding stable had been built just a few years ago, at the most.

The boy's eyes began to shine as he looked over the outside stalls with divided doors that led into separate areas where the animals could exercise any time of day or night.

Curious sorrels and black horses, which he was certain had cost fortunes, looked back at him.

But Logan was tired of walking through the stables under the staring eyes of all the riders. He stopped abruptly and whistled a loud, melodious tone, then looked around and listened.

When the whistle didn't work, he tried again and, from somewhere nearby, a whinny answered him.

Logan grinned broadly and then continued walking in the direction of the familiar sound. A few moments later, he was standing in front of Star, who looked at him with enormous but tired eyes and sniffed at him.

"Hey, boy! How was the trip? I'm really sorry I wasn't here when you arrived, but Mom held me up. I hope you can forgive me. Come here, Star boy. It's so great that you're finally here!" Logan's voice was as soft as butter as he talked to his horse, and it was clear how much he had missed him.

"Hey! What are you doing? Leave that horse alone!" A very unpleasant voice echoed through the stalls, but Logan couldn't imagine that it was meant for him. Lost in thought, he stroked the forelock on his horse's forehead, as he decided to allow him one or two days to rest up after the trip before saddling and riding him.

"I said, leave that horse alone! Get out of the paddock!" that brusque voice shouted again. It was obvious the man was pretty furious that someone had dared to enter the guests' stall area without asking.

Logan turned around, bewildered, as he realized that the red-faced man was yelling at him.

"Is there a problem?" he asked casually, placing his chewing gum in the other cheek, his hand still on his white Arabian's forehead.

The arteries in Nick Rizzo's neck swelled. The irate man felt provoked just by Logan's question, and he couldn't stand it when strangers poked around in "his" stalls.

His stalls?! Well, in a way, he felt responsible for everything that happened here at the riding club. He had been the head of the Board of Directors for many years, and had kept three horses at the stable.

"What's the problem?" asked Logan again, and looked condescendingly at the older man. "There can't be a rule against me visiting my horse, or is that forbidden here?"

"Your horse? What do you mean, *your* horse?" Rizzo began to stammer a little.

"Of course, *my* horse! My mother, Angela Bendix, paid for a stall three months in advance."

Rizzo's thoughts shot through his head and after a few seconds he remembered the nice woman, Angela Bendix, who had filled out the form for a guest stall some time ago.

The man looked the boy up and down, checking him out. He couldn't remember who had told him, but he recalled hearing that this kid had a reputation of being a loser – a rowdy, graffiti-painting guy who had caused a lot of trouble where he used to live and had had dealings with the police. Rizzo didn't know the details, but if he had known about the boy's background when Logan's mother had requested the guest stall for Star, he never would have approved it. After all, it was anyone's guess what the horse's owner might do here, and Rizzo was very committed to preserving the good reputation of the Avalon Riding Academy's stables.

Looking at Logan, he could hardly imagine that the boy had such a bad past but, nevertheless, Rizzo decided to keep a close watch on him. If he did anything wrong at all, he was going to throw him and his horse out of the stable.

"Oh, welcome. I hope your horse feels comfortable here." Rizzo forced himself to answer pleasantly.

"Thanks, I hope so, too!" replied Logan, and he turned back to Star, who was rubbing his huge head on the boy, almost making him lose his balance.

"I'm really looking forward to going riding with you, my boy," Logan told his horse tenderly. "But today I want you to rest, okay? And tomorrow, or the day after, we're going to have a look around the area."

* * *

Soon Ricki and her friends had reached the small woods that abutted Carlotta's Mercy Ranch.

The horses trotted between the trees on long reins with their heads hanging, and the riders guessed that the animals would have preferred to stay in their cool stable rather than be outside on this humid spring day, as much as they loved the outdoors.

"I'm starting to think that it wasn't such a good idea to make this detour to the ranch," admitted Ricki, apologetically.

"It's too late to turn back now, but I think that after we stop at the mill, we should ride back the shortest

16

possible way. It's so muggy now, riding isn't fun anymore. These big horseflies are almost eating the horses alive!" announced Cathy, swatting at them with her bandana, trying to rid Rashid of the bloodthirsty insects.

"We shouldn't have gone riding in the first place," agreed Lillian, who was wildly waving her arms around, fighting off a wasp that was threatening to get caught in her long hair. "Oh, this wasp is driving me crazy!" she growled, almost desperate. "I'm allergic to these things!"

She breathed a sigh of relief when the wasp finally flew away.

"Cathy, where did you put that fly spray that Josh brought us? I was going to spray Holli today but I forgot."

Josh, Lillian's boyfriend, whose father owned a riding shop in town, provided all kinds of free and useful things to his son's riding friends, especially if the packaging was damaged.

When Lillian hadn't received an answer to her question she turned around in the saddle and glanced at Rashid's rider, who was lost in thought.

"Earth to Cathy. Are you still here? Hellooooo!"

Startled, Cathy jerked out of her reverie.

"Sorry, I was somewhere else. What did you ask me?"

"Where did you put the fly sp–" began Lillian again, but Kevin suddenly interrupted her. "I bet Cathy has a crush!"

"What? You do?" Ricki looked over at her girlfriend in surprise. "Didn't you say that you never wanted to have a boyfriend again, after Lena took Hal away from you?"

"That's true. Kevin, you're crazy! Why would you even say that?" Cathy's face turned bright red.

17

"Very simple," explained Kevin. "The only time girls can sit and be quiet is when they like someone a lot. Therefore, my guess is you like somebody. You usually chatter from morning till night!"

"That's ridiculous!" Cathy stared straight ahead, embarrassed.

"Totally!" Ricki sided with her girlfriend. "Kevin, you're an idiot! It wouldn't hurt you to be quiet every once in a while either. But, Cathy, I'd like to know if he's actually right." Ricki stared anxiously at Cathy, who looked away, mad that Kevin had hit the nail right on the head.

In truth, her thoughts were with Logan at the moment, whose dark eyes had fascinated her right from the beginning. When he first entered Ms. Murphy's classroom, Cathy had the feeling that she was developing a crush on him. However, Hal was still around, and she just couldn't forget him, even though he had broken up with her. Her friends would think she was crazy if she told them her feelings were torn between the two, so she denied Kevin's suggestion outright.

"That's a lot of baloney!" she said heatedly, and wondered if her red face was going to give her away. "Kevin keeps trying to talk me into some relationship. I think it's really insensitive!"

The boy grinned broadly.

"If it's not true, why are you so upset?"

"I'm not upset!" responded Cathy, annoyed. *And anyway, there's no one around who would appeal to me,* she ended her sentence in her mind ... *besides Logan and Hal,* she thought to herself, sighing.

"Oh, Cathy, just admit it. There are a few guys who you would date, but not everyone likes girls who usually have the smell of horses in their hair," joked Lillian, too, as she bent way down over Holli's neck and stroked his mane between the ears.

"Exactly! So you just have to look for a rider," commented Ricki as she winked at Cathy. "Let's think who would be right for you. Well, there's –"

"Logan!" shouted Kevin, spontaneously. He snorted like a hippopotamus at his genius, which frightened Sharazan, who laid his ears back and began to prance.

"No! You can't suggest that guy for our Cathy," Ricki strongly objected.

"Why not?" asked Kevin, laughing and stroking his horse's neck to calm him down. "Just because you don't like him doesn't mean –"

"You know what? You guys are getting on my nerves!" Cathy shortened the reins and turned Rashid. "I don't feel like listening to you any more. See you. 'Bye!" And with that, she urged her horse into a trot and was soon a far distance from her friends, who watched her go in bewilderment.

"Hey, I think I hit the nail right on the head. She really does have a crush on Logan!"

"It looks like it."

"Or else all the talk about Logan got on her nerves, because she still has feelings for Hal," suggested Lillian.

Then the three of them rode on until they reached Mercy Ranch.

* * *

From inside the stable, Beth could hear her friends' voices as they arrived at the ranch.

19

Quickly, she shut Rondo's stall and ran outside.

"Hey you guys, what are you doing here? I thought; well, whatever! Good thing I've already groomed Rondo and now all I have to do is saddle him."

"Hi, Beth," Lillian greeted the girl. "Hurry up, will you? We have to ride over to the mill to order feed."

"I didn't know there was a mill around here." Beth looked at her friends. "Where's Cathy? Didn't she come with you today?"

Ricki shook her head. "She wanted to go on alone."

"Why?"

"Because I told her I think she likes that new kid in class, Logan," grinned Kevin.

"Oh." Beth's face turned a little darker, and Ricki groaned at the disappointment it showed.

"Oh, no! Don't tell me! Not you, too?"

"Hmmm, well, I'm going to saddle Rondo so that we can get going, okay?" Beth laughed to cover her embarrassment and ran back toward the stable.

"Oh, please explain to me what it is about Logan that has such a powerful effect on girls!" Kevin turned his face upward, toward the sky, in fake desperation.

Ricki objected. "Well, he doesn't have that effect on me at all."

"Thank goodness," Kevin smiled at his girlfriend. "I think I'd have something to say about that if he had."

Just then Beth returned with Rondo.

"Isn't Carlotta home today?" Lillian asked her. "She always comes out when we visit."

"She's brooding over her paperwork. She said she has

bills to pay and doesn't want to be disturbed," explained Beth. "But besides me, there isn't anyone here yet. The others are coming in an hour or so, I guess."

"Are Hal and Lena still together?" Ricki wanted to know.

"I think Hal already regrets breaking up with Cathy for Lena," Beth explained with a knowing smile, as she climbed into Rondo's saddle. "Honestly, just between us, she's really weird sometimes, and can be unbelievably nasty."

"Well," added Lillian, "a new girlfriend isn't always better than the old one. Hal should have thought about that before he made his choice. C'mon guys, we really have to get going. I can't stand this humidity, and I've got tons of homework to get back to."

Chapter 2

Jake had finished sweeping out the stalls and now stood leaning on the broom in the stable doorway, looking up at the sky anxiously.

"I just hope they get home in time," he mumbled to himself as he observed the dark clouds that were rapidly moving together to form a cloud cover.

Then, in the distance, he noticed a rider galloping lightly along the road toward the Sulais'. *Who is that?* he wondered, squinting.

"Hello, Jake!" he heard soon afterward. Josh, Lillian's boyfriend, pulled up riding on his pinto mare, Cherish. "Is Lillian here?"

"Oh, Josh! I saw someone coming up the road, but I didn't recognize you. Heavens, my eyes are getting weaker and weaker!" sighed Jake. "Anyhow, the girls and Kevin went riding."

The young man slipped down from the saddle and let the

reins fall to the ground, while Cherish, trained in Western riding, stood as still as a statue.

"Oh, darn. I finally have a day off and my girl is nowhere to be found. What a shame!"

These kids and their love lives! Jake smiled to himself.

"Lillian will be so disappointed when she gets back. Didn't she know you were off today?"

Josh shook his head.

"No, it just turned out that way. Mom took over my job in the shop today because she wanted to clean up. And there's no sense in both of us sitting around there. There aren't so many customers that one person can't take care of them alone." Josh took off his cowboy hat and hung it on the saddle horn, and then he wiped his forehead with a bandana he pulled from his back pocket.

"Phew, it's hot today!" he groaned. "I'm so wet I feel as if I've been swimming."

"Yeah, it's really muggy for this time of year. I think we'll be getting a thunderstorm soon. I hope the others get home before it hits. I never feel comfortable if they're out riding when a storm's approaching. Anything could happen." Jake chewed on his lower lip. "I shouldn't have sent them to the mill on a day like this."

Josh looked questioningly at the stableman.

"Our feed is almost gone, and I thought they could ride quickly over to the Kubitsch place."

"Oh, well, if they only rode to the mill, they should be back soon. After all, it's just –"

"If that's all they did, they'd be back by now," Jake interrupted Lillian's boyfriend.

"Hmmm." While Josh was considering whether to wait for the gang to return, he started rummaging around in his saddlebags, finally undoing the leather strap.

"Look, I brought you guys something," he said, and took out all sorts of things from his father's shop. "Saddle cream, hoof oil, two tie-up ropes ..."

"Did you loot the riding shop?"

Josh laughed.

"Not really, but the guy from the wholesale place was at the shop again today and he left us all kinds of samples of some new products. You have to take advantage of things like that."

Jake nodded absently.

He kept looking down the road, hoping the riders would appear, but as hard as he strained his eyes, there was no sign of a horse. However, within minutes the sky turned dark and a heavy rain began to fall. It was a real cloudburst.

Josh brought Cherish into the stable corridor, where she stood peacefully chewing at an opened bale of hay. Josh and Jake sat on a bench and talked, but the old man was restless and kept getting up to look outside.

"Jake, they won't come any faster if you keep running to the door every two minutes. How about we just –"

"Cathy's coming!" the old man interrupted him excitedly. "But where are the others?"

"What?" Josh jumped up, too, and went to stand beside Jake.

"I knew it! I sensed something had happened!" Jake nervously ran his fingers through his hair.

"Let's just wait and not get too upset yet," Josh tried to comfort Jake. "You'll see, there's probably a simple reason why Cathy rode home alone." Inwardly, he had to admit that he was a little worried. He hoped nothing had happened, to Lillian especially.

* * *

Cathy was relieved when she finally reached the shelter of the stable. Before Rashid had even stopped, she sprang from the saddle and pulled the animal inside.

"Ugh! What horrible weather!" Her glance fell on the empty stalls. "Aren't the others back yet?"

Jake shook his head, his lips pressed together tightly in concern.

"I was just about to ask you where they are."

"I have no idea. I didn't ride to the mill with them. Hi, Josh!"

The young man raised his hand casually in greeting.

"Since when do you guys separate on a ride?" Jake wanted to know.

Cathy pretended not to hear the question.

"They wanted to ride to Mercy Ranch first and pick up Beth."

"Oh, great! Don't you kids ever listen? I told you expressly not to make any detours because the weather was going to change." Jake sounded extremely agitated.

"Maybe they rode back with Beth and are waiting at Mercy Ranch for the rain to stop," Josh dared to suggest. "After all, the ranch is much closer to the mill than this stable."

Jake thought it over for a moment.

"That could be. I hope you're right."

"I'm freezing," complained Cathy, who was soaking wet. Josh helped her unsaddle Rashid.

"Then come over to my house, child, I don't want you

25

to catch cold," responded Jake who, without waiting for an answer, grabbed her arm and pulled her along. Cathy could take a hot shower at his house, and he had an old sweater of Ricki's lying around somewhere that she could put on.

"Josh, can you take care of Rashid?" called the old man over his shoulder.

The Western rider grinned.

"Of course," he replied and began to rub the dun horse's wet coat with straw to dry him off. However, every few minutes he would look out the window for the still missing riders.

* * *

Carlotta was just cleaning out the stalls with her young volunteers Hal, Kieran, Lena, Bev, and Cheryl, when Beth came back to the ranch on Rondo, soaked to the skin.

"Thank heaven, you're finally back," Carlotta said, relieved at seeing her.

"You can say that again. The rain and wind are freezing!" Beth shook with the cold.

"Didn't you see that a storm was coming? Why did you even go riding? I didn't see you leave."

"Ricki and the others picked me up about an hour ago. They wanted to show me around and they had to order some feed at the mill, so we rode over there. Up till then the weather was humid but fairly nice. Yeah, the sky was looking a little threatening, but we thought the rain would hold off until we got home. Unfortunately that didn't happen. Now I have to dry Rondo!" Beth led her gray Arabian gelding straight into his stall so that she could unsaddle and take care of him.

"You should put on some dry clothes, too," suggested Hal, as he was pushing the wheelbarrow with manure past Rondo's stall.

"I don't have anything with me!"

"You can put on my jogging outfit. It's lying on the bench over there."

Beth laughed.

"Did you bring that especially for me?"

"Of course!" Hal laughed in reply. "Actually, I wanted to go to soccer practice afterward, but with this weather I'm sure it'll be cancelled."

Carlotta came over to them. "Hal's right. Change clothes first."

"But Rondo ..."

Hal went into the stall and nudged Beth out.

"Back out. I'll rub Rondo dry."

"Oh, that's so sweet of you! Thanks a lot!" Beth slipped out and grabbed Hal's jogging outfit. "Carlotta, can I take a shower?"

"Yes, of course. You know where the towels are by now, don't you?"

Beth nodded and quickly ran off. She would be so glad to get out of these wet clothes.

Grimly, Lena watched her go.

"You take such good care of her," She hissed at Hal, as she went past him. "And you're so helpful!"

"That's just how I am. Helpful Hal."

"Maybe you'd like to help her shower, too," Lena's words oozed with sarcasm.

"Hey, what's your problem?" The boy looked at his girlfriend with huge, unbelieving eyes. "I'm only trying to lend a hand. What does it matter if I dry off Rondo and let Beth –"

But Lena didn't allow him to finish.

"Somehow the others always seem to be more important to you than I am!" she complained.

"That's not true!"

"Yes it is!"

"No it's not!"

"You always had more time for Cathy," the girl stated meanly.

"That's not true!" Hal said angrily. "Stop being so jealous!"

"I'm not jealous! But with Cathy you –"

"Hey, can't you just leave it alone? You're not acting normal anymore! I'm starting to ask myself –" Hal broke off in mid-sentence, and Lena looked at him angrily, ready for a fight.

"What is it you're asking yourself – why you didn't stay with that stupid cow?"

"That's enough, Lena!" Carlotta walked over to the girl and looked her sternly in the eyes. "This isn't a very attractive performance you're giving right now. You've really gone too far. Cathy never did anything to you. Just because she dated Hal before you doesn't make her a cow. And as far as I'm concerned, Hal did the right thing by giving Beth his jogging outfit, so that the child doesn't get sick."

"Child! Humph!" Lena mumbled to herself.

"Anyway," Carlotta paused dramatically, as her glance went back and forth between Hal and Lena, "if you want to pick a fight in the future, then please do it somewhere else, outside of my stable or, even better, far away from Mercy Ranch! I want peace and quiet here. Do you two understand me?"

28

Hal nodded, looking at the ground, embarrassed to be a part of the scene Lena had caused.

A few minutes later, Beth entered the stable through the connecting door to Carlotta's house.

"I feel great – like a new person!" she beamed. Then she held out the fabric of Hal's jogging jacket and laughed. "I look like a circus clown in this huge thing, but at least I'm not cold anymore. Gee, Hal, why do you have to be so big? ... Umm ... What's going on? You're all so quiet. Do I look that bad?"

"No. You look terrific!" Lena sneered at her before disappearing into a horse stall.

"Lena, I said that's *enough*." There was no doubting the severity in Carlotta's voice, despite her reserved tone.

Beth jerked in surprise and looked at the others, but Cheryl just rolled her eyes and Bev shook her head. Hal was still busy with Rondo, but his face was bright red. Only Kieran tapped his forehead and pointed to Lena, who was standing with her back to him.

Beth understood. Lena was having one of her hissy fits.

"I feel really sorry for Hal," she whispered to Carlotta, who continued to look severely at Lena.

"He chose Lena, so you have no reason to feel sorry for him," replied Mercy Ranch's owner, just as quietly. Then she cleared her throat and went back to work. At least her sermon seemed to have had an effect, because she didn't hear anything more from Lena the rest of the afternoon.

* * *

Ricki and her friends weren't far from home when they were surprised by sudden peals of thunder, followed by one flash of lightning after another lighting up the sky. Then the rain came.

They had a good ten more minutes to ride, but because the storm was getting worse they decided to wait out the rain in one of the Bates's sheds they were just riding past.

"I hate thunderstorms," said Ricki, as she stroked Diablo's neck comfortingly. The black horse stood tensely beside his owner, snorting through his nostrils nervously.

"Stay calm, my good boy. This storm will be over soon. Don't be afraid. Nothing's going to happen to you."

"Jake is going to have a fit. He must be worried to death because we're not home yet," reflected Lillian out loud.

"Me, too, if we don't get out of this shed soon," responded Kevin, casting a glance at the crooked roof of the old lean-to. "This thing looks like it's going to fall down any minute!"

"I've never known this shed to look any different. It's always been like this." chuckled Lillian.

"Oh, that's very comforting, isn't it?"

"I bet Beth got soaking wet, too."

"I'm sure!" Ricki risked a peek through the slightly open door. "It looks as though the rain has let up a bit. The thunder has moved away some, too. It's not right above us." She opened the creaking wooden door a little more.

Lillian stuck her head out. "It's hard to believe, but the sun is already out, and ... oh, get a load of that wonderful rainbow! Wow! It's great! You guys have got to see this!" She pointed upward, across the road. "I've never seen one with such intense colors before!"

"I think we should keep riding," suggested Kevin. "The next thunderstorm may be right behind this one."

"Yeah, you're right. We're already soaked anyway. Okay,

let's go!" Lillian, still enchanted by the rainbow, tightened her horse's girth and swung herself up onto Holli's back. All of a sudden she began to sing, "I'm always chasing rainbows ..."

"What's that about?" Ricki had to laugh.

"Don't you know that one?" asked Lillian, smiling. "It's a really old song by ... uhh ... Paul Anka or somebody like that, I think."

"By whom? Never heard of him!"

"My parents have it on an old record. Anyway, it doesn't matter. Let's get home! I'll be glad when we have the horses safely back in the stable! I for one am never going to doubt Jake's 'weather bones' again!"

"I hope Cathy isn't lost somewhere." There was concern in Ricki's voice.

"Oh, I bet not," Kevin tried to be reassuring. "She's probably sitting in the stable, dry and rubbing her hands with glee because we've been punished for our gossiping."

"Maybe," Ricki nodded, not really convinced.

Quickly the kids urged their horses into a trot, and soon they could see the Sulais' stable.

"Made it," Kevin said with a relaxed sigh when they had stopped their horses in the yard to dismount.

"Yeah, just in time. It's already as black as night up there." Ricki pointed to the sky and hurried Diablo into the stable.

"Well, thank goodness you're finally home!" Jake welcomed them. His voice sounded a little stern, but relief showed on his weatherworn face.

"Don't panic, Jake. We took shelter from the downpour."

"Hey, Josh!" Lillian lit up when she saw her boyfriend and his horse, Cherish. "Have you been here long?"

Josh wrapped his arms affectionately around his wet girlfriend.

"Hello, sweetheart. I've been here with Jake for about an hour and a half."

"Oh, so long? If I had known that –"

"If you had even thought that, you probably would have led us on a chase through the worst thunderstorm – never mind the lightning – just to get back here," Ricki joked. Then her glance fell on Rashid.

"Where's Cathy?"

"She took advantage of a short break in the rain and rode her bike home. I'm supposed to give you her love," said Jake.

"Really?"

"Yeah. Why do you ask?"

"Oh, no reason."

"Hmmm, I suppose I don't need to know everything that goes on with you kids," he grumbled, just a little insulted, and then he left to return to his cottage to make himself a snack while the kids took care of their horses.

* * *

The following days went by very quickly. There was school in the mornings and part of the afternoons, and afterward, since the weather was good, the kids were out riding and enjoying every moment of the warm spring.

While they rode they talked about everything. The only problem was that the conversation always went back to Logan, and always ended in a fierce debate. Ricki could not be convinced that their new classmate was a nice, likable, and definitely attractive guy, as Beth and Cathy constantly told her. But Ricki was stubborn, and sure that Logan was bad news, although she didn't know what kind.

"You're crazy," Beth said angrily one afternoon, and then refused to talk to her after that.

Cathy, on the other hand, just shook her head in disapproval. She couldn't understand Ricki's dislike of Logan either. After all, he hadn't given them any reason not to like him. However, when she thought about it, she just didn't care. Hal was much more on her mind, and seeing him always made her heart beat faster. Anyway, it was obvious that Beth had fallen head over heels for Logan, and nothing could be worse than when two friends both liked the same guy. Besides, Cathy sighed to herself, if one didn't stop having feelings for one guy, one couldn't be ready for a new relationship. So Cathy tried to put Logan out of her thoughts.

Lillian, on the other hand, couldn't say much about Logan because she still hadn't met him, and Kevin usually defended the guy, which Ricki didn't like at all.

"You're just being unfair," Kevin told her, and then an unpleasant argument wrapped the two of them in silence.

Lillian, who was a few years older than the others, had had enough of the couple's bickering and silent treatment.

"Hey, stop it you two. We're all supposed to be having a pleasant ride. If you don't cut it out right away, I'm going to turn around and ride home! The way you're acting is just too weird."

"I'll go with you," added Beth, immediately.

"Me, too!" burst out Cathy and then Kevin.

Ricki was left on her own, staring straight ahead before giving her friends a nasty look.

"Then go ahead! I can go riding by myself!" she shouted. Then she shortened Diablo's reins and let him gallop away.

Bewildered, the others watched her go and reined in their horses, who wanted to follow after the black horse.

"Whoa, Rashid! Calm down! I don't understand what's got into Ricki all of a sudden," said Cathy.

"Yeah, what's up with her?" asked Lillian.

Kevin shrugged his shoulders. "Why don't you ask me something easier."

* * *

Ricki didn't know what was upsetting her. She found her behavior strange too. She, who always looked for the good in people, kept obsessing about Logan, and suggesting all kinds of weird things.

Sighing, she reined in Diablo after a long gallop and looked back over her shoulder to see if the others had followed her.

Although she was relieved that none of her friends were close by, she felt a little hurt. At the very least she had expected Kevin to ride after her, but then she remembered that he had been angry with her, and she pushed out her lower lip in a pout.

"They'll see I'm right," she said softly to her beloved Diablo.

Chapter 3

Ricki had been riding alone quite a while when she met up with a friend from the Avalon Riding Academy where she, Kevin, Cathy, and Lillian used to hang out.

"Hey, Ricki! I haven't seen you in a long time. How are you?" Barb Bratton reined in her brown gelding, Giaccomo, as he came up to Diablo.

"Hi, Barb! Great to see you! I'm good," answered Ricki, her face lighting up happily. "Want to ride together for a while?"

"Sure! Hey, anything new happening? Are you still going out with Kevin? How are the others?" she asked, as the two girls rode side by side.

Ricki laughed. "That's a lot of questions all at once. Okay, first of all, yes, I'm still with Kevin, even though we're just ... " she paused, and Barb looked at her full of curiosity.

"Even though you're *what*?"

"Well, right now we have a few differences of opinion."

"Oh, relationship stress ... Ask Dr. Barb, she's always ready to listen."

Ricki shook her head.

"No, it doesn't really have anything to do with our relationship. Actually, it's stupid to be fighting about something like this, but ..."

"Ricki, stop beating around the bush!" Barb looked at her expectantly.

"All right. There's this boy, who –"

"So it *is* a relationship thing!"

"Barb, let me finish!"

"Okay. Sorry I interrupted you. Go ahead." Giaccomo's rider listened closely as Ricki took a deep breath and told her the whole story of her disagreement about Logan. When she had finished, Barb was silent for a moment as she regarded Ricki thoughtfully.

"Listen. A guy named Logan recently put his horse in the stable at the academy. Its name is Star and it's really a beautiful animal. But there's a lot of nasty gossip going around about the guy. He's supposed to have been involved in some thefts in New York City, and he's also rumored to be a notorious graffiti sprayer. There was also something about him hurting someone. Lately, they've been saying that he doesn't treat his horse very well. He overworks him when he goes riding."

Ricki's head jerked up.

"That's unbelievable! So my hunch that he's trouble is true."

"Like I said, it's just gossip, and I've only exchanged a few words with him. I really don't know him, but he seemed totally okay, I thought. But they say that Rizzo wants to throw him out of the stable, and as quickly as possible. You know Rizzo – 'Lowlifes have no place at my stable,' as he puts it."

Ricki nodded in agreement.

Since the new riding academy had turned private, and Nick Rizzo had taken over as head of the board of the riding club, only wealthy horse owners boarded their animals there. Ricki wondered how Logan had managed to get his horse in there. Rizzo was certainly not the kind of person whom people generally liked, but you had to admit that he made sure that in *his* stable everything was peaceful and orderly.

"Well, then I can't wait to see how long Mr. Bendix lasts!"

"Yeah, it's only a matter of time," Barb agreed, and then she reined in Giaccomo.

"Ricki, I'd really like to keep riding with you but, unfortunately, I have to get back. My grandmother turned seventy-three today and my parents and I are going to take out her to dinner to celebrate," Barb explained.

"Oh," Ricki was a little disappointed. She had been looking forward to talking with Barb a while longer. "Well, okay then. Have a nice time at the birthday dinner. I'll see you around, okay?"

"For sure. Take care, Ricki, and say hi to the others for me!" Barb turned Giaccomo around and waved good-bye over her shoulder, before she disappeared out of Ricki's sight in an easy trot.

Diablo whinnied loudly to Giaccomo, startling his rider.

"Hey, you! I'm sorry too that the two of them had to leave. Come on now, Diablo, it's time for us to be getting back, too." Lovingly, Ricki patted her black horse's neck and started for home. She couldn't wait to see how the others would take the news about Logan.

"That guy is starting to sound worse and worse," she mumbled to herself. That he was also apparently pretty rough with his horse shocked Ricki. She didn't like people who treated their animals, especially horses, badly. Diablo had belonged to a rough man who had mistreated and hurt him, until Jake saved the animal and then finally gave him to Ricki as a gift.

Just as she was reminded of Diablo's suffering, a tidal wave of affection for him filled her heart. Spontaneously, she bent way over in the saddle and wrapped her arms around her horse's neck.

"I'm so glad I have you," she said softly to him, and, as happened so often, she couldn't imagine her life without him.

"You two were made for each other," she recalled Jake's words, and a feeling of pride and happiness overwhelmed her.

Diablo was really special. Well, it was probably the same for Lillian with Holli, Kevin with Sharazan, and Cathy with Rashid, but still ... there was a very unique closeness between Ricki and her black horse. Sometimes it seemed as though the horse could read the girl's mind and act accordingly, and the bond that connected the two of them also meant that Ricki could sense when something wasn't right with her horse.

"You two definitely are soul mates," Lillian had said recently, when she was standing at Ricki's window looking down at the paddock. Ricki had just glanced at Diablo and immediately his head flew up, he turned toward her and he whinnied loudly to her.

Ricki breathed deeply before turning her thoughts back to the present.

Every rider should be soul mates with a horse, she thought and tried to imagine what kind of relationship Logan had with his horse.

He probably doesn't have one, if he overworks it, she decided, and her new classmate became even less appealing.

Impulsively she steered Diablo in another direction, and soon she was on the trail that Barb and Giaccomo had ridden not too long ago.

But something had forced her to ride to the stable where Logan's horse was boarded instead of returning to her own stable.

* * *

" ... And even if you say I'm guilty a hundred times, IT WASN'T ME!" said Logan, his voice trembling with rage. Star, who was saddled and standing behind him, snorted nervously and jerked his head at his owner's angry voice.

"It's okay, boy," Logan tried to calm his horse and pulled slightly on the reins.

Nick Rizzo stood in front of Logan and stared at him, both hands resting on his hips, his eyes full of anger.

"Who else could it have been? No one here besides you has the reputation of being a troublemaker and a graffiti sprayer. And no one can say that I don't give everyone a chance to improve, but I should have known that someone like you would never change!"

"Yes, I admit I spray-painted back in New York, but that doesn't automatically mean that I sprayed this mess on the walls of the stable, and I don't have anything to do with your flat tire!" Logan tried again to defend himself, but Rizzo just waved his objections aside.

"Strange, but before you came, everyone here was peaceful and happy. But in the few days since you've been here things have happened that I won't tolerate!"

"Okay, but why should I take the blame? I mean, you're not loved by everyone here either! Did you ever think that somebody else might have enjoyed slashing your tires?" burst out Logan. Rizzo's face turned purple, and the man looked as though he was going to explode.

"You're not only a loser, you're impudent! An impudent brat! I'm going to tell your parents about your behavior and inform them that you will have to pay for the cleaning of the stable wall and for a set of new tires. In addition, you'd better start looking for another place to stable your horse!"

Logan shook his head in disbelief, closed his eyes for a moment before he opened them again, and wondered if he was having a bad dream. Then he turned on his heel, and pulled Star after him.

I have to get out of here, he thought. *Just get out of here before I forget myself and say something worse to that idiot!*

As fast as he could, he left the stable with his horse, and Rizzo followed him out. A few riders standing around in the parking lot observed Logan leaving and, whispering, pointed at him.

"One week! Do you hear me?" Rizzo shouted after him, his voice screeching. "I'll give you one week to find another place to board your horse, and then I don't want to see you around here anymore!"

Logan mounted Star in a flash, and pressed his calves against his body so that the Arabian galloped off instantly, crossing the courtyard and heading straight toward a path through a neighboring field.

"Ever heard of warming up your horse before you gallop?" Rizzo screamed after the boy. "You're a disgrace to every rider, in addition to ..."

Logan didn't hear what other horrible things the head of the riding club shouted after him. He just stared straight ahead and was glad that Star was taking him farther and farther away from that revolting man, who had accused him so unfairly. Only when he was out of sight did he rein in his horse and stroke his neck with his trembling hand. He felt guilty about Star. Of course he knew that you should warm up a horse before you gallop! That was the only point on which he agreed with Rizzo completely, but ...

"Please, forgive me, boy, but I couldn't help it. That Rizzo is such a disgusting jerk and I couldn't stand being near him and listening to his accusations another second," said Logan softly, his voice shaking. He asked himself yet again who could have repeated the information about his past, and who could possibly benefit by saying things against him right from the start in this new town. But no matter how hard he thought about it, he couldn't think of anyone here who would have told such lies about him.

* * *

Ricki had been a few yards away from the Avalon Riding Academy when she saw the stable door rip open and Logan storming out of the building with Star, followed by Rizzo.

41

She stopped Diablo suddenly and had been an unwilling witness to Rizzo's last few angry sentences as well as Logan's rapid departure on Star.

Rizzo's words still echoed in her head: "One week ... then I don't want to see you around here any more ... You're a disgrace to every rider."

A disgrace to every rider. Ricki thought about it. Rizzo couldn't have been referring only to Logan's riding style. No! Something else must have happened in the stable. Maybe Logan had beaten his horse. At any rate, Ricki got very upset as she imagined all kinds of other horrible things that Logan might have done. More than ever, she was sure that she hadn't been wrong in her judgment of her new classmate's character.

Quickly, the girl turned her black horse around. Now all she wanted was to ride back home as fast as possible, so that she could tell the others the news about Logan.

Hah! And Kevin thought I was just being mean, she thought triumphantly. *Now he'll have to take that back*!

* * *

Hal sat like a little pile of misery in Carlotta's office.

"I just don't know what to do. Lena is getting more and more impossible to be around. She wasn't always like that, was she?"

Carlotta sat behind her desk and looked at her helper for a long time.

"Do you mean her jealousy?"

"Yeah, that too. Just imagine, now she's furious with me for going riding with Cheryl. That just isn't normal!"

"Jealousy is a terrible thing, Hal. It can destroy everything.

I just think that she's scared of losing you, and she doesn't realize that she could do just that with her jealousy. But apart from that, she is a very domineering girl and she likes everything to go the way she wants it to."

"Oh, yeah, that's the truth!" the young man agreed. "She's started talking like a drill sergeant, and that makes it really hard to like her."

"Hal, if you don't mind my asking, why aren't you with Cathy anymore? She's such a nice girl, and she has her heart in the right place. Why did you trade her in for Lena?"

Hal blushed. "Well, you can't call it that ... 'trade' sounds really bad!"

"Okay, then you tell me what to call it."

"Love?"

Carlotta made a face.

"Hal, I saw you and Cathy together and there was definitely a very special closeness between you two. If I look at the situation today, then I have to say that you and Lena don't give the impression of teenagers in love. You fight all the time, and usually over small, unimportant things. I'm amazed that you aren't both tired of it!"

"But what should I do? She's so demanding. I can't just say yes to everything, can I?"

"No, Hal, you shouldn't do that, but what do you expect me to tell you?"

The boy was silent and Carlotta looked pensive.

"You're hoping that I'll tell you clearly whether or not you should break up with Lena, right?"

Hal nodded hesitantly.

"I can't do that, Hal. That's something only you two can

decide. I can only advise you to look at your relationship objectively, and then listen to your heart to see if Lena's the one. If she is, then sit down with her and talk to her about everything. But if it's not serious – let's say you just like her – then end the relationship before you two tear yourselves apart and, in time, upset everyone here at the ranch."

Hal groaned as though he were burdened with something enormous, and then he got up slowly.

"Do you know that I miss Cathy?" he asked softly, sniffed, and went out. Carlotta watched him go and observed him for a long time after.

I'm glad I'm no longer a teenager, she thought. *The path to becoming an adult isn't easy, especially when you can't understand your own feelings. But every young person has to go through these experiences in order to grow up.*

* * *

For a long time, as they rode home, Beth, Lillian, Cathy, and Kevin talked about Logan, and the more they talked, the more Beth liked the boy, no matter what Ricki thought of him. Ricki's opinion was no longer important to Beth. She decided to find out if Logan had a girlfriend back in New York.

"Someone that cute definitely has a girlfriend," the girl said out loud.

"Good looks aren't everything!" responded Cathy, and got a grumpy look from Beth.

"You're starting to sound like Ricki."

"I am not. I just meant that caring about someone isn't just about liking how he or she looks. It's also about two people being on the same wavelength."

"That's true. But, oh, I hope he's still single," sighed Beth.

"You should just be direct and ask him," Kevin suggested. "Then you'll know for sure."

"I wish it were that easy!" Beth had such a tortured look on her face that her friends started to laugh.

"Good grief, Beth, just tell him that you're crazy about him!"

"I can't!"

"Why do you girls think that we guys always have to make the first move?" asked Kevin. "In every other way, you're so emancipated!"

"Oh, I don't know!"

"Well, I thought it was romantic when Josh asked me if I wanted to go out with him," commented Lillian.

"I felt the same way with Hal," said Cathy softly, with sadness in her voice.

Silently, the friends looked over at her and they knew that Cathy's feelings for Hal were not gone.

There was a crossing in the path up ahead, and as they approached it, Beth said, "Hey, I'm turning off here, or I'm never going to make it home before dark. Besides, I have to find the way back to Mercy Ranch by myself, and I don't know my way around very well yet."

Beth said her good-byes and set off with Rondo. "I'll see you all tomorrow at school."

"Yeah, so long!"

"Later!"

"'Bye!"

* * *

After the long conversation with her friends, Beth's head was buzzing, and she enjoyed being on her own and riding back by herself.

"This is great, isn't it, sweetie?" she said to her horse as she stroked him lovingly across the top of his mane. Dreamily, she looked down at her gray Arabian, who held his head aloft elegantly, even though the reins were long and his mane waved back and forth in rhythm with his steps.

Beth was overwhelmed with feelings of pride and happiness. Rondo was really beautiful, and she couldn't imagine loving any other horse more than she loved him. She felt the same way Ricki felt about Diablo. Oh, yes, Beth was thrilled when she first saw the wonderful black horse; however, there was no way she would ever trade Rondo for him, even if she could.

"You are the best horse in the world and you always will be!" she whispered to her gelding, who listened, playing his ears back and forth so that he could hear what his rider said.

For quite a while, lost in her thoughts, Beth just rode straight ahead, until she discovered a little path that led directly into the woods, one she had never ridden on before.

"Let's see where this goes," she said quietly to her horse and steered Rondo toward the path.

Oh, this is so beautiful! she thought. As the sun shone through countless trees onto the path, other than Rondo's hooves there was absolutely nothing to hear but the calls of various birds. Overcome by the magic of the forest, Beth thought that there was almost nothing more wonderful than riding through the woods.

When she reached the next fork in the trail, she stopped to get herself oriented. This place seemed familiar to her.

"Oh, I remember!" she murmured to Rondo. "We were

here a few days ago with the others. If we keep to the left, we should come out on Echo Lake."

Rondo scraped the ground in boredom.

"All right! We're moving on!" she said, laughing, and she loosened the reins and pressured Rondo's sides with her thighs so he surged ahead.

As they picked up momentum, Beth could sense the unexpressed power of her horse beneath the saddle. "You'd think you hadn't been out in weeks," she said affectionately.

"Let's get you some exercise!" she said, and allowed him to gallop.

After they galloped for a while, she saw another rider in the distance, galloping in her direction, so Beth gently but firmly pulled back on the reins to make Rondo slow down.

Logan noticed the other rider almost too late, and he was just barely able to get Star to slow down.

"Oh, sorry," he called out. "I didn't see you! The sun ... "

"Yeah, sure, it's the sun's fault," grinned Beth, and her heart gave a huge leap as she recognized the rider. "Wow, Logan, you have a beautiful Arabian. Is he yours?"

"Yeah. This is Star. Your Arabian isn't bad either!"

"His name is Rondo," said Beth, proudly, blushing.

"Oh, nice name."

The two horses stretched out their necks and looked each other over critically for a few seconds. Then, maybe because they were the same breed, they seemed to decide that they could be friends.

"Where are you headed?" Logan wanted to know.

"I want to ride past Echo Lake."

"If that's the lake with the neighboring nature preserve,

then that's where I just came from. There are a lot of people there."

"Really? Then maybe I'll just turn around and ride home another way. I don't feel like being around a crowd of people right now," said Beth.

Logan looked at the girl whom he had already noticed at school. She was much more interesting here, sitting on her horse.

"If you want to, we could ride together for a while," he suggested.

"Sure, why not?" Beth turned Rondo around and tried to act as indifferent as possible, although her heart was beating excitedly.

Oh no, I think I'm going to die! What am I going to do if Logan notices that I am insanely, madly nuts about him? What am I going to do if –

"Do you know your way around here?" the boy interrupted her thoughts.

Beth said no.

"I haven't lived here very long yet."

"Oh, so you're new in school too, huh?"

"You could say that."

For a while the two of them rode side by side in silence, both feeling unsettled.

"Rondo boards at Mercy Ranch. That's a ranch for old and neglected horses," Beth said all of a sudden, but actually only to say something before Logan could guess her innermost secret thoughts. "Actually he's there only temporarily, until I find another stable. The ranch doesn't have any official boarding stalls."

"At the moment, I have Star at the stables of the Avalon Riding Academy, but let me give you a piece of advice. Don't even think about boarding Rondo there. The people are awful!"

"Really? It's a good thing you told me. I had thought to ask about a stall there. It's not so easy to find a good stable, is it?" sighed Beth.

When Logan didn't react, she tried again and couldn't help but remember all the things Ricki had said about him earlier that day.

"Hey, what's wrong? You look so weird all of a sudden. Did you ... did you have problems at the riding stable?"

"Kind of ... Why?"

"Well, it just sounded as if you're looking for a stable, too, even though your horse has only been there for a short time," suggested Beth. But she turned away quickly when Logan stared hard at her.

"Do you believe all that stuff they've been saying about me, too?" he asked suddenly, directly, his voice becoming slightly aggressive.

Beth took a deep breath. "I have no idea what you're talking about."

"You don't?"

"No!"

"Good, then let me tell you!" And while Logan fixed his gaze straight ahead through Star's ears, everything that had been bothering him for so long just burst out: his mistakes in New York City, the things Rizzo had accused him of, and the fact that he now had only a week to find a new stable for his horse.

When he had finished, he stopped Star and looked straight into Beth's eyes.

"And? What do you have to say now?"

"Nothing," the girl managed to say. What she had just heard sounded like a bad movie.

Wordlessly, Logan's eyes stayed fixed on Beth, as her thoughts raced through her head. She was unable to say anything and tried first to sort out everything she had just heard.

When she didn't say anything, Logan just shrugged his shoulders, urged Star on and rode off, without even looking back at the girl.

When he was a few yards away, Beth woke up, as if she had been in a trance.

"Logan," she called after him, softly at first, then a little louder. "Logan, Wait! Hey, I don't think you did what Rizzo said!"

"And why not, after all I told you about New York?" he asked after a short pause.

"I just don't!" Beth urged Rondo into a light trot so that she could catch up to Star. "You told me everything. I think if you were really guilty of the things that happened at the stable, like the graffiti, you wouldn't have told me anything, or at least you would have put a different slant on it."

Logan swallowed. "Thanks," he said softly. "You're probably going to be the only one who believes I'm innocent."

"Better one person than no one," answered Beth and put her hand on the boy's arm. "Hey, don't be sad. I'm sure they'll find the person who really did it!"

Logan laughed bitterly.

"It's just a question of whether they'll find him in time, before Star is out on the street."

"Oh, gosh, yes ... Star. You need a new stable for your horse more than I do." Beth slapped her hand on her forehead.

"I only need one temporarily," said Logan then. "In three or four months our stable at home will be renovated. There are four stalls because we're planning on boarding three other horses so Star won't be alone."

Beth looked at him with enormous eyes.

"That sounds great!"

Logan nodded.

"It is great, but it doesn't help me right now." He looked at Rondo's rider for a long time. "Umm, if you want, you can look at the stable sometime when it's finished and, if you like it, you can decide if you want to board Rondo there."

Beth's head jerked around and her eyes began to shine as she looked at him in surprise.

"Really? Are you serious? That would be fabulous! Thanks for the offer, Logan! That's really nice of you!"

"Yeah, sometimes I am nice, even though no one believes it," he said softly with an ironic undertone that made Beth's heart ache. She would have liked to give him a hug at that moment, to show him that she thought he was much more than just nice, and also because she had the feeling that it would be good for Logan, and ...

"Well, I don't know which direction you're going to ride," Logan interrupted her thoughts, "but I'm going to turn off up there to the left which will take me back to the stable. Since I don't know my way around here that well yet and I still have to find the right path, I think it's better if I start back now."

Beth nodded, disappointed.

"That's too bad," she said, and her voice sounded sad. "I have to ride straight ahead, but maybe we can go riding together again sometime!" she said with a warm smile that found its way directly into Logan's heart.

"Sure! Maybe even tomorrow?" he asked, and all of a sudden he sounded hopeful.

"Okay, why not?! See you at school tomorrow!" Beth said good-bye and waved to Logan.

"Yep! Until tomorrow then!"

The girl stared at the rider for a long time as he rode off.

"And they said he's a bad guy," she murmured. "It's true, he's done a lot of stupid stuff in the past, but I'm sure he regrets it now. I think he's sweet, don't you, Rondo?"

The horse began prancing nervously on the path as Logan and Star disappeared behind the trees at the fork of the road, but when Beth rode on with Rondo, he quickly calmed down.

"That Rizzo guy sounds really weird. If only I knew how to help Logan," Beth thought out loud. Suddenly her face lit up.

"Of course! That's it! Rondo, hurry up – we have to get home!" Beth urged her Arabian into a fast trot. She almost couldn't wait to get back to Mercy Ranch. She had to speak to Carlotta!

Chapter 4

When Ricki returned to the family's stable, her friends were no longer there. Jake told her that they already had tended to their horses and ridden their bikes back to their own homes.

She was disappointed that she couldn't tell them then what she had found out about Logan, but it would have to wait until tomorrow, at the bike stand before school began. Unfortunately, the next morning Ricki overslept and had to race to get to class before the bell rang.

Beth was sitting next to Logan with an angelic expression on her face, while he seemed almost unapproachable. That didn't bother her, although she did complain to her friends later that he didn't even answer her good-morning greeting.

"What's with her this morning?" Cathy whispered to Ricki, motioning with her head toward Beth.

"I have no idea, but I do have something to tell you

later! You won't believe it, but I was a hundred percent right about Logan!" Ricki whispered back.

Cathy rolled her eyes. "Oh, please, not that topic again, and so early in the morning. Spare me anything to do with Logan. I have my own problems."

"What's wrong?"

"Still the same thing – I can't stop thinking about Hal!" she managed to say before Mr. Walters, their math teacher, rushed in and without warning plunked down a piece of paper in front of each student.

"Good morning, everyone! Put your books and notebooks away. Here we go – you have half an hour for this test."

A general groan went through the rows of students.

"Quiet, please! Everything you say now will be used against you." Mr. Walters joked, but no one was laughing.

Beth bent over to put her notebook in her backpack and leaned her head toward Logan.

"Hey, I found a new stall for Star!" she whispered quickly to him, before sitting up again.

"What?!" Logan burst out in disbelief, staring at his neighbor. "Say that again."

Beth nodded in confirmation and smiled at the boy, but when Logan took a breath in order to reply, Mr. Walters got mad.

"I said, 'Quiet'! That means you, too, Logan! If I hear another sound from anyone, that person will get an automatic failure! Do you understand me?"

With that threat, the students quieted down, and soon their heads were brimming with math questions.

* * *

The test was barely over when Logan jumped up from his seat, grabbed Beth's arm and pulled her aside.

"Tell me! Is it true? You found a stall for Star? Where? At whose farm? How did you ... ?"

Beth laughed.

"Well, pay attention. Actually, the idea hit me right after we said goodbye yesterday. I ... "

Ricki looked disapprovingly at the two of them.

"I have to talk to Beth, later," she murmured quietly to herself, as she saw her friend and Logan engaged in an intimate conversation.

"I don't believe it!" Shaking her head, she watched Logan wrap his arms enthusiastically around Beth and give her a kiss on the cheek.

Cathy, on the other hand, responded rather casually. "Well, it looks like the two of them are a couple." She sighed loudly and found her thoughts flying directly to Hal. She missed him so much!

"That's not going to turn out well!" prophesied Ricki, but before Cathy could say anything else, the break was over and Beth sat back down, a dreamy look on her face.

"I have something to tell you!" Ricki whispered to her. Beth looked over at her briefly.

"I have something to tell you, too!"

* * *

"I can't believe it!" Ricki said repeatedly, getting more and more upset. She had been brushing the same place on Diablo's coat for at least five minutes but didn't even notice. "Beth is bringing that Logan and his horse to Mercy Ranch, even though he just got thrown out of Rizzo's stable! Carlotta is going to have a fit. I doubt that Beth told her about Logan's history."

From across the backs of their horses, Lillian, Kevin, and Cathy gave each other one of those *here-we-go-again* looks.

"I can tell you this – what Barb told me and what I saw are enough to –"

"Cut it out, Ricki! You're starting to get on our nerves! If only I knew what's making you so weird! This obsession with Logan just isn't natural!" Kevin looked at his girlfriend, shaking his head. He was tired of hearing Ricki talk about nothing else but Logan.

"I mean, first of all, why do you care what Logan may or may not have done? Second, we all know by now that you don't like him, so you don't have to keep reminding us! And third, your rants are becoming unbearable!"

Ricki's head jerked around.

"Thanks a lot! How come you're being so mean to me?" she asked her boyfriend unpleasantly.

"I just can't listen to this stuff anymore, and I don't feel like dealing with your attitude. No one would. Anyway, haven't you ever done anything wrong that you regretted afterward?"

"Come on, you two, stop fighting and make up." Lillian tried to mediate, but Ricki threw her brush in the grooming basket and began saddling Diablo as quickly as possible.

"Maybe you guys don't care if that guy hangs around Mercy Ranch and does who knows what, but I'm going to ride over to Carlotta's and tell her everything I know about Logan."

"And what exactly do you know? You can't believe that Logan ... "

Ricki didn't hear what Lillian said because she was already

leading Diablo out of the stable and, jumping into the saddle, she rode quickly in the direction of Mercy Ranch.

Back in the stable, Ricki's friends looked at each other with puzzled expressions.

"If she keeps this up, she's going to have to look for another boyfriend," threatened Kevin, seriously annoyed. Then he turned back to Sharazan. Ricki's strange behavior was really getting to him. He asked himself why his girlfriend couldn't think of anything but Logan. It made Kevin even more upset that Logan was better looking than he was.

* * *

Beth had promised Logan to meet him halfway between the Avalon Stables and Mercy Ranch, after Carlotta had given her okay to moving Star into the stable, so she was just saddling Rondo when Hal turned up.

"Hey! Where did you leave Lena?" asked Beth, innocently, as she buckled the snaffle.

"I have no idea where she is," Hal said, his voice strained.

"Uh-oh, more stress?"

"Still!"

"Oh, you poor thing! By the way –"

"Hal?" Lena's voice echoed through the stable before Beth could even finish her sentence. "Are you here?"

"Where else would I be?" the boy mumbled. "See you later, Beth. Enjoy your ride."

"Thanks! Later! Oh, could you please open the gate to Rondo's stall?"

"Sure!"

"Hal? Oh, there you are!" Lena looked back and forth

between Hal and Beth. To her, they looked like accomplices to a secret, and it made her mad that she couldn't figure out what was going on.

"Hi, Beth!" she said coldly. "Did you two have a good talk?"

"Sure! We *always* have good talks! Bye, see you later!" responded Rondo's owner, and she walked past Lena, shaking her head.

At that moment Beth couldn't decide who annoyed her more; Ricki, whom she had argued with after school about Logan, or Lena with her constant jealous scenes.

"Both of them are crazy," Beth decided in the end as she mounted and seated herself in Rondo's saddle. Then she set those thoughts aside so she could focus on Logan. She was so happy that she was going to see a lot more of him when Star was in his new stall at Mercy Ranch.

* * *

Logan's imminent departure was greeted with general relief at Avalon Riding Academy.

Nick Rizzo stood in front of the tack room and watched Logan with eagle eyes as he packed up his things, to make sure he didn't take anything that didn't belong to him.

"I'm sorry that it has to come to this, young man, but I hope that at least you will have learned something from all this," Rizzo called after him as Logan shouldered his backpack, in which he had stowed Star's grooming kit, and moved past the chairman of the board.

The boy stopped a moment and slowly turned toward the man he hated.

"So, you're sorry," he said slowly, his voice trembling.

"You're sorry that my mother almost had a nervous breakdown when she heard what you were accusing me of. You're sorry that she cried for an entire day, although it wasn't necessary! That's great! You've really done a fine job! Thanks a lot!"

"It was necessary!"

"No it wasn't, because I'm innocent of all the things you accused me of doing here, but you don't believe me anyway!" Logan looked at Rizzo with red-hot anger, and then he ran to Star, who stood saddled in the corridor of the stable.

"Come on, boy, there's no reason for us to stay here any longer!" Logan walked past the gathering riders with his horse, and all of them stared at him with deep dislike. Rizzo had done his work well.

They're all morons, Logan thought, and he was glad to finally mount and ride away. He never looked back. *Hopefully, Beth is right about Carlotta Mancini.*

"And, if not, Star, then we really have a problem."

* * *

After arriving at Mercy Ranch and putting Diablo in one of the guest stalls, Ricki went straight to Carlotta's house. She sat on the same chair Hal had sat on when he had talked to the ranch owner about his girlfriend problems.

Without wasting any time, Ricki began to tell Carlotta all she knew about Logan, also expressing her worries about what could happen at Mercy Ranch if Carlotta decided to accept Logan's horse in the stable.

"I bet Beth didn't tell you anything about him, because you would have rejected her request," ended Ricki, taking a deep breath. Now that she had gotten all that off her chest she felt better.

Carlotta listened to her attentively without interrupting once, which actually had made Ricki feel a little awkward. When the girl finally finished, Carlotta stayed silent and thoughtful for a few minutes before responding.

"You're wrong, Ricki," she began slowly. "Beth did tell me some things about this Logan: all of the rumors that are going around and also facts that she heard from the boy herself. It was important to her that I knew everything, as much as possible, about the situation. Even though she hasn't been here long, she knows that I expect everyone who goes in and out of here to be open and honest with me."

"What?" Ricki looked at Carlotta with surprise, her eyes wide. "You knew everything and you're still taking the risk that –"

"Now stop right there, Ricki!" Carlotta interrupted. "You know that the wellbeing of horses is the most important thing to me, and if Logan needs a stall for his Star for a few weeks, because otherwise the horse will be left homeless, then I don't have to think about it for long. I'm not doing anything I didn't do for Beth, who also needed a temporary stall for her Rondo."

"Yes, but –"

"But nothing. Ricki, you heard some things from others and you saw some things, but you don't know any of the background. You know me well enough to know that I always make my own judgments about others and never care about what other people say or think about them." Carlotta paused, "And I thought you did the same."

Ricki turned bright red.

"Nevertheless, I'm very grateful to you for your good

intentions in trying to save me from difficulties. Really, child, I am, but I think you've let your imagination run away with you!"

"That's what the others said to me," the girl admitted softly.

"Well, if that's the way it is, then maybe you should rethink some of this, don't you?" Carlotta smiled and affectionately put her hand on Ricki's. "Don't worry so much, my dear. I promise you that I will keep a close eye on Logan. And let me give you a bit of advice – never draw conclusions from situations you don't know much about or listen to rumors that could hurt someone. Sometimes people make others into what they *want* to see in them. Do you understand?"

Ricki nodded, dejectedly.

When she left the office a little while later, she really intended to take Carlotta's words to heart, but she also decided to keep her eye on Logan. She just couldn't – or wouldn't – admit to herself that she could have been so wrong about him.

She went over to the stable, mulling over what Carlotta had said, and ran into Hal, who was just getting a stall ready for Star.

"He's supposed to be a great horse, if you can believe what Beth says about him," he said, grinning.

Ricki shrugged her shoulders.

"I can't say. I only saw him once, briefly." Indifferent, she went into Diablo's stall to saddle him for the ride back home.

"You're not staying?" asked Hal.

Ricki shook her head.

"I have to get home. I still have homework to do," she lied and occupied herself with Diablo's snaffle.

Hal stepped over to her horse's stall. With a glance over his shoulder to make sure that Lena wasn't nearby, he discreetly cleared his throat.

"Ahem ... How's Cathy? Is she okay?"

Thrown by Hal's concern about her friend, Ricki turned to face him.

"She's okay. Why do you ask?"

"Well, I ... that is ... oh, Ricki, I think I made a huge mistake ... with Lena, I mean."

Ricki couldn't help grinning a little.

"It's nice that you've realized that yourself. Do you want to know the truth? Cathy is suffering terribly because she still cares for you, a lot. So, now you know. You can do what you want about it."

Hal, feeling a combination of sadness and relief, stepped away so that Ricki could get past him with her horse.

"You think I could ... I mean ... "

Annoyed, Ricki looked back at Hal.

"I don't know!" Everything was just too much right now. Because of Logan she was fighting with her girlfriends, had lost Beth's friendship, was having problems with Kevin, had gotten a lecture from Carlotta, and now Hal was bothering her with his relationship stuff.

Ricki felt as if her head was like a dimming lightbulb, and she was glad when she was finally on her way home on Diablo. Depressed, she glanced down at her black horse's neck, rocking back and forth.

"Tell me, am I really such an unfair monster? Or am I just crazy?" she asked him, and then she bit her lower lip hard, as though Diablo had given her an answer she didn't want to hear.

She went home a different way because she was pretty sure that Lillian, Cathy, and Kevin were on their way to Carlotta's ranch, and she didn't want to run into them right now. She was too ashamed of her behavior over the last few days. Why did she feel so awful about herself right now? And why did she have the feeling that, other than Diablo, there was no one else in the world who understood her?

* * *

Beth met Logan as planned, and now the two of them went on their way to Mercy Ranch.

"How did your parents react to Rizzo's call?" Beth wanted to know.

"My mother cried pretty hard, but luckily she believed me rather than that moron." Logan looked over at Beth.

"Have I thanked you yet?" he asked.

A slight blush appeared on the girl's face.

"I think so."

Logan smiled. "You are really nice, you know that?"

Now Beth didn't know what to say at all, but her heart was beating wildly as she met Logan's gaze.

"I think I like you," he said softly, and the girl felt so giddy with happiness that she thought she might faint.

"I like you, too!" she replied, hoarsely.

Logan stopped Star and looked at Beth.

Oh, wow, those eyes! Unbelievable! she thought, and then Logan leaned over and kissed her gently on the cheek.

"Everything okay?" he asked then, and Beth nodded, smiling. At that moment she was incapable of saying anything, but she could have hugged the whole world – that's how happy she was.

* * *

Hardly half an hour after Ricki left Mercy Ranch, Kevin, Lillian and Cathy arrived, and when Hal saw the three riders through the stable window, he felt a lump in his throat.

Cathy! He inhaled deeply and decided to talk with her, but Lena was already standing nearby, watching with anger as Hal's former girlfriend arrived.

"Why does she have to keep coming here?" she asked spitefully.

"Because Rashid belongs to Carlotta, remember?" Cheryl responded from Jam's stall.

"That's no reason!" The sting of jealousy bored deep into Lena's heart, especially when she saw that Hal had left the stable and was acting as though she wasn't even there.

"Hey, Hal! Is Star here yet?" shouted Lillian.

"No."

"Hi, guys!" Cheryl had come out, too. "Say, what did you do to Ricki? She's is such a good mood!"

Kevin caught the irony in Cheryl's teasing and just shook his head.

"Stop it, will you?"

"Uh-oh," reacted Cheryl, and ducked her head in fun. "I guess I should just stick to asking you about the weather," she winked at him.

"Storm clouds are moving across an otherwise blue sky, and we can hope that the storm is over soon!" laughed Lillian, looking at Kevin.

"There's been a hurricane called Ricki for a few days now. I know why these horrible storms get girls' names!" Kevin said, glancing over at Hal.

64

The two boys grinned at each other in mutual understanding, without saying another word.

Hal was just about to turn to Cathy, who was stroking
Rashid enthusiastically, so that her ex-boyfriend wouldn't
notice how much her hands were shaking, when Cheryl
pointed to something in the distance.

"I think the new horse is coming. I'll tell Carlotta!"
Then she ran back to the house.

* * *

"Everyone at Mercy Ranch is really nice!" said Beth
reassuringly, for the zillionth time, as she noticed Logan's
face getting more and more tense the closer they came to
Carlotta's stable. "Well, almost everyone. Lena is mean,
but it's bearable."

"And you told Mrs. Mancini all about me, really?"
asked Logan. "I mean, not that I –"

"Carlotta knows everything, and don't worry. If she
hadn't had a good feeling about you, then you wouldn't be
on your way there right now. She's really great. You'll see,
you'll like her!"

Suddenly Logan straightened himself up in the saddle and
squinted his eyes. "Isn't that Kevin and Cathy there in the yard?"

Beth followed his gaze.

"Yeah, it looks like them. And Lillian! What a curious
bunch! They all want to see your Star," she smiled broadly,
and was really glad that she couldn't find Ricki in the group.

"That's almost like an official reception!"

Silently the two rode on until they brought their horses
to a halt in front of Carlotta, who, in the meantime, had
come out of her house.

"Welcome to Mercy Ranch!" she smiled at Logan. Immediately, he jumped right down from the saddle and reached out his hand to her.

"You must be Mrs. Mancini," he said pleasantly. "Thank you so much for letting me bring Star here!"

"This is Logan," introduced Beth.

"That's what I thought," teased Carlotta and nodded to the boy. "Hal fixed up a stall for you. Maybe you should take your horse into the stable first. We can talk later." She turned to Cheryl. "Please, would you unsaddle Rondo? Beth, come with me, if you will."

With a questioning look, the girl handed over Rondo's reins to Cheryl and followed Carlotta back to the house.

"Is something wrong?"

"Probably nothing earthshaking," answered Carlotta, stopping on the porch and turning to the girl. "Ricki was here a while ago."

"Oh, no!"

"Tell me, what's going on between you two?"

Beth lowered her gaze.

"She's stressing out!" Then she began a defense of Logan, until Carlotta, laughing, waved her talk aside.

"Enough, enough! I can see, even without your detailed explanations, that you like him a lot."

Beth blushed.

"But I'm worried about Ricki. Do you know if she's having any problems? I mean, besides the fact that she doesn't like Logan?"

"Oh, I have no idea."

"Hmmm," Carlotta mulled over Beth's reply before she

left the girl and went into her house. She had the feeling that Ricki was hiding something, and that was the reason for her present behavior. But, of course, it was possible that she was wrong.

I need to have another talk with her when I get the chance, thought Carlotta, and she decided to think it over some more with a strong cup of coffee. Maybe it could help her figure out what was bothering Ricki.

* * *

While Carlotta was waiting for the coffee to brew, the kids were all standing around Star's stall admiring Logan's white Arabian.

"How old is he? Have you had him for long?" Hal wanted to know.

"He's seven years old, and I've had him for three years now," Star's owner told them proudly.

"Oh, Arabian horses are just fabulous," added Beth, glancing at her Rondo. "But I think every kind of horse, even the mixed breeds, have a certain something, and really, it doesn't matter. All horses are sweet!"

"That's true." Cheryl looked at Sheila, the horse she took care of, and sighed. "Still, your favorite horse is always the most beautiful and the best one of all. Oh, if I could, I'd buy Sheila right now."

"But she's just like having your own horse, isn't she?"

"Yeah, she is, but it would be different somehow if I knew that she really belonged to me!"

Cathy nodded knowingly. She felt the same way about Rashid, but the chances that she would ever be able to own him were about a million to one. All of a sudden, she felt a light touch on her shoulder and, without turning around, she knew that Hal was standing behind her.

"Please, Cathy, can we talk?" he asked softly.

"Why? What is there to talk about? You chose Lena, and I have to accept that, even if I don't understand it," she replied, though not feeling as sure of herself as she sounded. Cathy felt Lena's gaze on the back of her neck, despite the fact the girl wasn't even in the stable. She straightened her shoulders and forced herself to take a few steps to the side, trying to act indifferent. She just couldn't talk to Hal right now, even though there was nothing else she would rather do.

Chapter 5

The next two weeks went by quickly. Star adjusted well to Mercy Ranch and Logan felt at home there. As for Carlotta, she had no complaints about the boy. He was always helpful to her and the others, and had become a welcome member of the group of volunteer helpers. Every time he arrived at the ranch they all rushed to greet him and, for the first time in his life, Logan felt he had found real friends, friends that were there for each other without having to prove anything.

On the other hand, Ricki's relationship to her friends was still pretty tense. She spent more time alone with Diablo riding through the countryside than ever before, while Lillian, Cathy, and Kevin got together almost daily with Beth and Logan to go riding. Hal frequently joined them, which angered Lena, who knew that the others didn't want her around. In order not to lose face, she kept finding things to do that made it impossible for her to go along with them, although they never asked her to join them. She usually stood in the stable entrance, her hands balled into fists and grinding her teeth, and watched Hal leave on Jonah, riding next to Cathy. Lena seemed like a powder keg ready to explode at any moment.

Her jealousy grew day by day, and she would have liked to send Cathy to the moon or someplace even farther away from Hal, whom she knew still had feelings for Cathy.

* * *

"I think Ricki doesn't like me any more," Kevin announced one day, as the kids were riding around Echo Lake.

Surprised by his confession, Lillian asked, "Why do you say that?"

Kevin shrugged his shoulders. "It's just a feeling." Then his glance fell on Logan. "Ever since you came into our class she's been acting so weird. At first I thought she had a crush on you."

Logan laughed out loud.

"Ricki? A crush on me? That's a joke! She doesn't even look at me! Anyway, she didn't like me right from the start. And after everything Beth told me, she's never going to accept me. But I don't care." He hesitated a moment, before he continued. "But, I have the feeling that she's always watching me out of the corner of her eye, especially when she's at the ranch. Do you know what I mean?"

"No."

"Oh, I can't really explain it ... it's like she's waiting for me to screw up or something. It's just so weird."

Kevin was taken aback.

"She's been coming to the ranch? Then why isn't she riding with us?"

70

"She usually disappears just before you guys get there," said Logan.

Kevin stared straight ahead. If only he knew why Ricki was acting so oddly.

* * *

A downcast Ricki sat on a bale of straw after her ride and watched Diablo munching contentedly on his hay.

Jake came strolling along the stable corridor and when he saw Ricki's moody expression, he paused and leaned on his broom, considering what to say to her.

"Are the others still out riding?" he asked indifferently, as if he hadn't noticed that three stalls were empty.

Ricki nodded without looking over at him.

"It's been a long time since you all went riding together. Is there a reason for that?" he asked, but all he received as an answer was a shoulder shrug.

"Are you guys fighting?"

Further silence.

"Well, if you communicate with your friends like you do with me, then it doesn't surprise me."

"Oh Jake, can't you just leave me alone?"

"I could, but I don't want to," the old man countered stubbornly. "You're mad because you've realized that you were wrong about Logan and you can't admit that to the others."

Ricki's head snapped up.

"What do *you* know about it?"

"I heard more of your fight than I wanted to. After all, you guys were pretty loud."

The girl stared at him.

"Ever since Logan came everything has been about him," she burst out suddenly. "He's so good looking, his horse is so fantastic, he's so nice! Beth and Cathy are wild about him. Beth became his girlfriend, by the way. Lillian always has a ball with him, and Kevin seems to have sealed a pact with him. Logan this, Logan that! No one says anything about what he did in New York and how he acted at the Avalon stable! And Carlotta accepts a guy like that at Mercy Ranch with open arms! I don't get it! I'm so sure he's going to make trouble at the ranch but nobody believes me!"

Jake put his broom aside and stood in front of Ricki with his arms folded in front of his chest. The teenager seemed to stare right through him.

"Ricki, be honest with yourself," he said slowly, choosing his words carefully. "You have never judged anyone because of their past, yet now you're doing just that with Logan. It sounds more like you're jealous because your friends like him so much, and you're looking for a reason that they won't find him so great anymore."

"That's crazy!"

"No it's not. And what's worse is that Kevin's found a friend in Logan, whom you don't like."

"That's not true!"

"I think it is."

Ricki jumped up.

"Why does everyone think I'm the one who's mean? I don't understand it!" Feeling terribly hurt, she ran outside.

"You aren't being judged by anyone, Ricki," Jake called after her, "but maybe you should think about how you appear to your friends." Then he walked over to Diablo's stall and stroked his forehead.

"My boy, be glad you're not a human. We make problems for ourselves that aren't really problems."

* * *

Cathy avoided Hal whenever she could. It was bad enough that he always tried to be near her when they went riding, and the idea that he wanted to talk with her made her panic. What could he possibly want to say to her? Did he want to explain why he was now dating Lena?

No thanks! I don't need that! the girl thought, as she stormed into the tack room to get her fanny pack, which she had left there before going riding.

Unfortunately she ran right into Lena, who was standing beside her best friend, Bev, and gesturing wildly with her arms. When Cathy entered, they both stopped talking immediately and looked at her angrily, but before they could say anything Carlotta appeared and waved two envelopes in the air.

"Cathy, would you please take these two letters with you? You go past a mailbox on your way home, don't you?"

Cathy nodded.

"Of course, I'd be glad to. Put them down here," she pointed to the small metal cabinet, where the various salves and ointments for the horses were kept. "I have to wash my hands first, so I don't get the paper dirty."

"Good, but don't forget them. It's important that they get mailed today. If these letters don't get there on time, I'll have problems."

"What problems?" Logan came through the door to hang up his saddle equipment.

"Mine, if the documents aren't at the I.R.S. the day after tomorrow at the latest," Carlotta answered freely. "Actually I wanted to bring them to the post office myself, so I could get a receipt, but I just can't get away today. There's money in the other one. I know, it's not a good idea, but I'm late paying Mr. Kubitsch for the feed and my online banking site isn't working, so this one time I'm sending him the money."

"I hope the letter carrier doesn't steal the money. There was one who opened letters at Christmastime in order to 'earn' himself a little extra cash," Bev commented.

"Let's hope not. That really wouldn't be good," Carlotta answered, and then she put the letters on the cabinet and went back to her office.

"Cathy, where are you? We have to get going," Lillian called from the corridor.

"Coming!" called Cathy, as she tried to clean the grease from her fingers under the cold-water faucet.

* * *

"Star must have stumbled on the paddock this morning, and now he's limping a little," Logan greeted Beth with the news the next day at Mercy Ranch.

"Oh, then you can't come riding with us?" she asked sadly. Logan shook his head.

"No, sorry."

"What if you took one of Carlotta's horses?" Beth asked hopefully, but Logan said no again.

"No, I don't want to do that."

Beth thought it over a moment.

"Then I'm not going riding today either."

"Don't be silly! Of course, you're going riding!" He

gave his girlfriend a hug. "I promise I'll still be here when you get back."

"Promise?"

"Definitely! I think I'll use the time to wash Star's tail and dress it. It's really about time I did it."

"Okay. Then I'll groom Rondo and get him saddled. I'm going to meet the others at Echo Lake and I'm already running a little late."

"I'll help you with Rondo, so you can leave sooner," Logan responded without thinking, and he ran to the tack room to get the brush and comb.

* * *

The next day, Ricki waited until Lillian, Cathy, and Kevin had ridden off before she went over to the family's stable to saddle Diablo.

She hadn't slept well the night before, once she had decided to have a talk with her friends in the morning. Her guilty conscience concerning her behavior toward them was making her feel worse and worse. She just couldn't allow everything to be destroyed by that Logan.

However, when she went to meet her friends that morning in front of the school, Beth and Logan were wrapped tightly together beside the other three, so she couldn't say anything. She wanted to talk to them *without* Logan around, so she just walked past them and said a faint hello. And now, when she could have had a chance to talk with them in the stable, she was feeling so bad that she decided to put it off again.

Ricki looked at her watch. If she waited another ten minutes, she could be sure she wouldn't run into them on her ride. Actually, she didn't want to ride to Mercy Ranch today, but Hal had called her up and pleaded with her to meet him there.

"This whole mess with Lena is killing me. Cathy keeps avoiding me, and since you're her best friend, I thought – Oh, please, Ricki, come over. I have to talk with someone."

I need someone myself to tell me what to do right now, Ricki thought, and she leaned against Diablo's neck, sighed, and closed her eyes.

"Somehow, everything is completely messed up! Oh, Diablo, I wish you could speak," she said plaintively. Then she opened the gate to his stall and led her black horse outside.

As she was riding away, she felt terribly alone and neglected. She missed going riding with the others and she knew it was her own fault that she had excluded herself.

"Maybe Jake was right," she whispered to Diablo. "Maybe I am jealous. Maybe Logan isn't such a bad guy, and I'm just too stubborn to admit it."

Diablo's ears played back and forth attentively. He sensed that something was wrong with his rider, because her inner turmoil was gradually transferring itself to him. He kept shying at little things that otherwise wouldn't have bothered him. Just the shrill sound of a crow was enough to make him jump to the side, and Ricki, lost in her own thoughts, almost fell out of the saddle.

"Hey, hey, what's that all about? Are you trying to get rid of me?" Startled, she sat back up straight in the saddle as she was determined to pay more attention during the rest of the ride.

A short time later she arrived at Mercy Ranch, and just as she was about to dismount, she saw Logan, who was pouring out a bucket of water.

"Oh man! He's here!" she said quietly to Diablo and was almost tempted to ride back home, since she really didn't want to run into him today. But at the same moment, Hal came running over, waving to her.

"Ricki! I'm so glad you came. I'm really grateful. I just don't know what to do."

Taking a deep breath, she slid down from the saddle.

"Hey, Hal. It's fine ... Umm ... the others ... Why didn't Logan go riding with them today?"

"Star is lame."

"Oh." Ricki's look got a little darker. Was it possible that Logan hadn't warmed up his horse again and just galloped away from the stable? Ricki didn't stop to consider that a harmless stumble could have caused Star's lameness. She was so sure of what had "really" happened that she didn't bother to ask.

On the other hand, Hal was too deep in his own thoughts about Cathy to notice something brewing in Ricki's head.

"Come on," he said, instead. "Bring Diablo into the stable. I thought we could sit down behind the riding ring and talk without anyone disturbing us." Right after saying that, his lips silently formed the word LENA. It really was too bad that his jealous girlfriend was always in the stable. It was almost as though she followed him everywhere and spied on him.

However, at the moment, Hal's bothersome girlfriend was nowhere to be seen, so Ricki hurried to settle Diablo

77

into a guest stall before the girl could show up and prevent Hal from having his important talk.

Less than ten minutes later, Ricki and Hal ran over to Carlotta's riding ring, and sat down in the shade of a big, ancient tree.

But someone else also was looking for some peace and quiet – Logan.

Ricki frowned when she noticed him, sitting a short distance from them. After he had looked around a few times, he reached into his pocket and brought out a wrinkled envelope, and then he seemed to be deeply engrossed in its contents.

"He could have found somewhere else to go," complained Ricki, but Hal just waved her objection aside.

"Oh, come on, he doesn't bother me at all!" he said, and took a deep breath. Somehow it was really hard for him to find a beginning to what he wanted to say, but as soon as he began to speak, the words seemed to flow out of his heart, and Ricki listened closely.

"Why don't you just break up with Lena, if she's getting on your nerves so much? I mean, if all you're doing is fighting, then it isn't worth staying in the relationship, right?" Ricki said after a while.

"That's true, but you can't break up a relationship just because you're fighting."

"If you only fight sometimes, then of course not, but if it's all the time, then it's not worth it anymore."

Hal sighed. "With Cathy it was completely different," he said wistfully.

Ricki made a face.

"Good grief, Hal. Are you aware that you keep thinking about Cathy? Cathy this, Cathy that. Why aren't you two together anymore?"

"That's what I keep asking myself."

"Terrific!" mumbled Ricki. "You're a real idiot, Hal, you know that? You're still stuck on Cathy, aren't you?"

The boy had a hard time speaking.

"I ... I don't know ... Could be ... Maybe ... "

"Well, at least that was a clear answer," Ricki said sarcastically. "Can you please tell me why you're sitting here with me and not with Cathy? Maybe it would be better if you talked it over with her. I definitely have the feeling that you two have a lot to talk about."

"That's all I can think about, but Cathy won't let me near her. I've already tried to talk to her, but she keeps avoiding me. But ... do you think that Cathy still cares for me after all that's happened?"

"Of course!" Ricki answered, without taking a breath.

"I really regret breaking up with her for Lena. Cathy is so sweet."

Ricki nodded.

"And what's keeping you from telling her that, without going all around the barn first?"

Hal was so confused, he couldn't answer. He knew he had to make a decision, because the way his life was now with Lena was simply unacceptable. Her terrible jealousy and their daily fights got on his nerves so much that he was considering not even going to Mercy Ranch anymore.

"I think you're right!" Hal said suddenly. "This just

can't go on! Lena's behavior is killing me, and it has nothing to do with love. I think I made a huge mistake."

"What do you mean, 'You made a mistake?'"

Hal took his time to answer.

"Maybe it has something to do with the male ego," he tried to explain. "You have a nice girlfriend, and suddenly you realize that there's someone else who likes you, and you feel terrific because now there are two girls who are interested in you... And then you begin to play with fire. You imagine what it would be like to be with the other girl. You think about which one of the two of them would better, and then, before you're aware of what's happening, you want to know."

"And then?" asked Ricki, her voice hoarse. Suddenly she thought of Kevin. She wondered if he sometimes had similar ideas.

" ... And then ... then it can happen – you choose the wrong one! Unfortunately, it's like in chess ... if you touch a piece, it's a move! You've made a move and you can't take it back when you realize that it was the wrong move. You have to keep playing the game until the end. That's really awful, because you're only allowed to rethink your move and then move your pawn somewhere else, if you have an experienced or generous opponent. Do you understand?"

Ricki nodded. "You're the pawn in this game, aren't you?"

Hal nodded, too.

"Yeah, and I can only hope that Cathy is a generous partner, who will give me another chance, if I ask her!" Suddenly he bent over to Ricki and grabbed her hand.

80

"You wouldn't believe how glad I am that I talked to you. I think a lot of things have cleared up thanks to this conversation, and I think I now know what I have to do!"

Ricki smiled, although she had a lump in her throat.

"I'm glad I could help out, and I hope everything works out for you, for both of you!"

As they stood up, Ricki thought to herself, *I hope Kevin isn't the kind of chess player who has to satisfy his ego like Hal did. I don't know if I could stand it if he suddenly appeared with someone else!*

Immediately, she decided to have a talk with her boyfriend. She was aware that in the last few weeks she had behaved badly, and that wasn't a very good basis for a relationship that meant everything to her.

Automatically, Ricki looked over her shoulder at Logan, who was still sitting in the shade of the trees. She still didn't like him and she thought it was his fault that she wasn't getting along with her friends.

I'm going to get home quickly. I hope I can saddle Diablo before Logan gets back to the stable, she thought to herself, and her face darkened.

And someone else frowned and bit her lips until they almost bled.

Lena had been watching Hal and Ricki from the stable window and had seen Hal reach for Ricki's hand. She wanted to come running out and make a scene, but she held herself back. *What was that guy thinking?!*

Instantly Lena knew that she had to make sure Cathy could no longer come to Mercy Ranch. Only then would she have Hal to herself. If only she knew how to manage it.

"I have to get to Mercy Ranch!" said Cathy suddenly, after getting a text message.

"Huh? Why? I thought we were going to ride around Echo Lake today," responded Lillian confused.

Cathy blushed. "Hal just sent me a text message," she said.

"Oh, does the lost darling suddenly miss you?" asked Kevin, sarcastically.

"He wrote that he still likes me and wants to break up with Lena."

"What?"

"Well, I think he wants us to get back together, if he writes that he likes me," replied Cathy softly.

Beth looked at her thoughtfully.

"And what about you? Don't tell me that you're just going to take him back with open arms after what he did to you?"

Rashid's rider sniffed loudly.

"Oh, but I still like him, too!"

"Well, then, let's get to the ranch," grinned Kevin. "Lena will be furious!"

"Oh, gosh." Cathy looked really hesitant.

"You have to do this," responded Lillian.

Beth agreed, saying, "She's not going to eat you. I think she'll probably want to get out of there."

"Let's hope so," sighed Cathy with mixed feelings, although her heart was beating wildly with happiness. Just the idea of being together with Hal again allowed her to forget all the sadness and hurt she had felt during the last few weeks, although she wasn't sure she could so easily forget Hal's being with Lena.

* * *

The riders had soon changed direction, and after only half an hour, they could see Mercy Ranch in the distance.

"If I get back together with Hal, then I'll invite everyone out for ice cream," Cathy promised.

"How? Don't tell me that you got a raise in your allowance?" grinned Lillian.

"No, but my grandma gave me some money," winked Cathy happily. But suddenly she felt very nervous.

"Please, guys, don't leave me alone," she pleaded, when they finally reached the stable.

"Don't worry, I'm sure Hal has already talked to Lena."

"Do you think so?"

At that moment Hal came out of the house as though they had called him, and waved to Cathy from a distance, beaming happily.

"Hal! I want to go home! Are you coming?" they heard Lena calling.

"Uh-oh ... it doesn't look as though he told her after all!" Kevin slid out of Sharazan's saddle, curious how it all would turn out.

"Only a movie is better than this," he said quietly, and got a nasty look from Lillian.

"Don't be so unfeeling," she whispered to him.

Before Hal, who was ignoring Lena's calls, reached Cathy, Carlotta stuck her head out of the window.

"Oh, Cathy, come here for a minute, please."

The girl jumped down quickly from Rashid's saddle and gave Lillian the reins, and then she waltzed past Hal with a smile on her face.

"I'm coming. What's up?" she called and stopped short under the window.

"I want you to come here with Rashid tomorrow afternoon. Dr. Hofer is coming to vaccinate all the horses and we can do your darling, too."

"Okay. When should I be here?"

"About four o'clock would be fine."

"Good!" Cathy was just about to turn around when Carlotta held her back.

"Did you mail the letters?"

The girl gave a start.

"Oh, no, I completely forgot about them. Oh, gosh, Carlotta, I'm so sorry. They must still be in the tack room. I'll go get them right away."

Carlotta frowned unhappily.

"I told you how important they are."

"I know." Cathy lowered her eyes with remorse.

In the meantime, her friends had come over to her and were following the conversation silently.

"I'll –"

"No! I prefer to do it myself!" Carlotta interrupted, and Cathy felt as though she had been slapped, even though it was justified.

The whole time, Lena stood leaning against the wall near the entrance to the stable.

"Lena, run to the tack room and bring me the letters," Carlotta told her, but Lena pushed herself away from the wall and slowly walked over to them.

"I can't," she said broadly, while Cathy looked at her from the corner of her eye.

"What do you mean, you can't?" asked Carlotta with annoyance.

"Well," the girl cleared her throat and replied, "They're not in the tack room anymore. I saw Cathy put them into her jacket pocket yesterday."

"What?" Cathy looked incredulously at her. "That's not true! We left so quickly yesterday that I forgot the letters."

Lena shook her head slowly.

"I'm really sorry, Cathy, but I saw you!"

Carlotta's look went back and forth between the two girls, then her voice took on a sad tone.

"I have the feeling that one of you is lying to me. I don't know which of you is trying to fool me yet, and I don't know why, because you're not just hurting me if the letters don't get where they're supposed to go – you're hurting the ranch and especially the horses!"

She took a long pause before continuing, her intense gaze boring into the two girls. "Maybe you'll think this over again. In the meantime, I'll have to drive to a copy shop and photocopy the papers for the I.R.S. again, and then I'm going to take my letters to the post office myself. Since there was money in one of the envelopes, which was intended for the horses' feed, it would be very good if at least that envelope turned up again!" Then she stepped back and shut the window.

Logan had joined them in the meantime, too, and Beth, whispering, told him quickly what had happened.

Cathy turned as pale as a ghost, and she slowly turned to her friends.

"I swear I didn't take the envelopes!" she said tonelessly, before she turned to Lena, completely overwhelmed.

"How could you say that you saw me taking them?" she asked her, her voice trembling. "That was a detestable lie!"

Lena folded her arms on her chest.

"I saw what I saw," she replied stubbornly. "After all, we heard Carlotta say that there was money in the envelope. Who knows what you needed it for?"

"That's ... that is simply ... Lena, you're awful! You accused me of stealing! That's unbelievable! As if I –" Cathy couldn't find the words.

Helplessly, she glanced around and noticed the questioning looks her friends were giving one another. Cathy sensed exactly what her friends were thinking, and the idea that they could actually believe she had stolen something, even though they didn't say it, almost made her break down.

Shaking her head, she began to sob and rushed over to Rashid, tore the reins from Lillian, mounted as quickly as she could, and urged the dun out of the yard.

"Hmmm, if that isn't a confession, I don't know what is," Lena said with a self-satisfied look, and glanced over at Hal.

"Be quiet, Lena!" Hal said, in an unusually severe tone of voice. "I'm pretty sure I know who's lying – and it's not Cathy!"

"Hah!" responded the girl, shrugging her shoulders and turning to go back into the stable, obviously indifferent.

"What now?" asked Beth.

Lillian and Kevin looked at each other.

"We should ride after her. She's really upset," answered Lillian, and Kevin nodded. They swung themselves back up into their saddles, but before they could turn their horses around, Hal stood beside Kevin and looked up at him.

"Please, tell her that I'm crazy about her, and ... and that I don't believe she did it!" he pleaded.

"I'll do that. 'Bye, Hal."

Lillian and Kevin hurried after Cathy, who was already out of sight. Knowing their friend, they figured she would probably just ride around aimlessly, so it was best to catch up with her as fast as possible. They were sure she felt awful, and neither could believe that Cathy had taken Carlotta's money, even though it was strange that she'd said she had come into extra money that very same day.

Chapter 6

Upset by her conversation with Hal and about her own situation, Ricki rode all over the area hoping to run into her friends after all. She felt it was incredibly important to talk to them today to clear the air. But it just didn't work out the way she'd hoped, and, eventually, after failing to meet up with her friends, a disappointed Ricki rode back home.

Lost in her thoughts, she was just brushing Diablo's coat dry when Cathy led Rashid into the stable.

"Hey, I didn't notice you coming back," Ricki said, in her old before-Logan friendly manner, and smiled at her friend. However, her smile faded when she saw Cathy's red, swollen eyes, and knew that her friend had been crying. She looked at her questioningly, but Cathy remained silent.

"What happened? Did something happen to the others? Where are Lillian and Kevin?"

Cathy shrugged and began to unsaddle Rashid with her back to Ricki. All of a sudden, she felt a hand on her shoulder.

"I know that I've been really awful lately, Cathy, and I'm truly sorry," apologized Ricki. "But if you have any problems, and you want to talk about them, I'm here for you."

Cathy brushed away the new tears that were beginning to form.

"Carlotta thinks that I stole some money," she said sadly. Then, hesitantly, she told her the whole story, as Ricki listened in horror.

Cathy hadn't yet finished when Kevin and Lillian returned just in time to hear the last sentence.

"Lena is lying! I didn't take the letters!" Cathy sobbed, completely overcome.

"Hal asked me to tell you that he believes you and that he still likes you," said Kevin, uncomfortably, as he looked at the tearful Cathy.

"Thanks. But that doesn't help me right now!"

Ricki put her arm around Cathy's shoulder, and now encircled her in a comforting hug.

Lillian stood back, looking at Cathy, and one could see there was something bothering her that was difficult to say. Taking a minute to find the right words, Lillian slowly began.

"Cathy, I don't think you took the money, but you must admit it's a little strange that exactly on the day you invited us all for ice cream –"

Instantly Cathy whirled around to face her.

"Can I help it if my grandmother gave me twenty dollars yesterday? She was visiting us, and I was totally down because of Hal and stupid Lena. Grandma gave me the money and told me to go shopping to buy myself something nice, so I wouldn't have to think about those two for a while. I know that sounds like an excuse now, but I swear, it's the truth. I got the money from her, even if you don't believe me, and ... and I'm not a thief!"

Awkwardly Cathy freed herself from Ricki's hug and led Rashid into his stall before rushing out of the stable, getting on her bike, and pedaling home as fast as she could.

"Did you have to say that?" Ricki asked with annoyance.

"Maybe not," answered Lillian, obviously upset. "But if I hadn't said it, I probably would have choked on it. It just wouldn't give me any peace."

Ricki didn't respond; she seemed to be thinking about something ... and suddenly it all became clear.

"I think I know who took that money." she said slowly.

"You do? But you weren't at the ranch when Carlotta put the envelopes on the medicine cabinet."

"No, but today Hal said he needed to talk to me, so I rode over there. We talked, and I saw Logan –"

"Oh, no! Are you starting with Logan again?" Kevin interrupted his girlfriend angrily. "That's unbelievable! Now you're saying he's a thief, aren't you? Listen, Ricki, don't you see that your Logan-bashing is really getting on our nerves? So it's Logan's fault again, and probably only because you can't stand him!" Ricki's behavior was really bugging him.

"I saw him sit down a little bit away from us and open an envelope," she started explaining again, this time without letting Kevin distract her. "He sat there with it for a long time and kept looking around as though he wanted to make sure no one was watching him!"

"You *what?*" Lillian looked at her with disbelieving eyes.

"If Cathy is under suspicion, I have to talk to Carlotta about this," said Ricki.

"And you're sure? I mean, maybe he was just sitting there and –"

"I'm sure!"

Lillian and Kevin exchanged a quick glance, and then they looked doubtfully at Ricki.

"I know that you two are mad at me and don't believe me because of the things I've said about Logan," stammered Ricki. "It's understandable ... but I did see Logan with an envelope!"

"I guess it would have been possible for him to take the envelopes after Cathy forgot them – if she really forgot them!" responded Kevin slowly. "He was in the tack room, too, when Carlotta explained what was in the envelopes."

Uncertain, the three friends stood silently looking at one another.

"But Lena said that she saw Cathy putting them in her pocket."

"Hmmm, but she could be lying because she doesn't like Cathy and wants to get her in trouble."

"I think it's all very mysterious!"

"Maybe the envelopes just fell behind the cabinet and are still there," suggested Lillian.

"That's possible, of course. But I think we should ride over to the ranch tomorrow and look around. If the envelopes aren't there, then I'm going to tell Carlotta what I saw." Ricki undid the rope from Diablo's halter and led her gelding into his stall.

"Cathy would never steal anything," she said with conviction, before the friends parted for the day.

* * *

When Ricki met the kids in front of the bike rack the next morning before class, Beth, who had already heard from Lillian and Kevin what Ricki said she'd seen, yelled at the girl like a madwoman.

"You're crazy, Ricki Sulai, making Logan responsible for the theft! Just because you don't like him doesn't mean you can start false rumors about him!"

"But I –"

"Oh, stop it! I don't have to listen to you! If you want to make trouble for Logan, you're going to regret it! Just leave him alone!" Beth gave her a warning look before putting on her backpack and storming off toward the school entrance.

"Did you guys have to tell her everything I said?" asked Ricki, understandably upset. "I thought we were going to have a look around first to see if the letters are still behind the cabinet."

"Apparently Carlotta thought of that last night, but she didn't find anything. Beth told us herself this morning."

"Oh," responded Ricki. "Then maybe my idea isn't far from the truth after all. Maybe that's why Beth was so freaked out."

* * *

In the afternoon the friends got their horses ready to ride over to Mercy Ranch. Cathy would have liked to stay home, but since Rashid was going to be vaccinated, she had to go with them. The closer she came to the ranch, the more awful she felt, and Lena's nasty smirk, which greeted her as she entered the stable with Rashid, didn't make her feel any better.

"Hey, Cathy! Did you spend the money already?" Lena asked spitefully.

"You know I didn't take it!" responded an angry Cathy.

"You're forgetting that I saw everything!"

"You're lying!"

"You can't prove that!"

Cathy looked at the girl with contempt.

"You're not going to get away with this!"

Lena smiled confidently.

"I wouldn't bet on it!" Then she quickly left the stalls.

"You little lying rat!" uttered Cathy after her. "What did I ever do to you to make you tell such lies about me?"

"Hi, Cathy." Hal, who had come out of the tack room, was suddenly behind her. That's when it became crystal clear to Cathy what she had "done."

* * *

Carlotta had listened attentively to Ricki's details of yesterday, and now she sat in her office thinking it over.

The whole situation surrounding the missing envelopes was bothering her a lot. Not that she couldn't have managed despite the money that had disappeared – it hadn't been that much – but the fact that she felt she couldn't trust the kids who came and went on her ranch made her extremely sad.

After all, she wanted to create not only an oasis for horses, but also a place for young people to enjoy their love of animals and feel at home. She was always a good friend to the kids and a good listener to all their problems, big and small. She had trusted them completely, and they had never abused that trust until now. Because of that Carlotta had to consider Ricki's suspicions about Logan. Perhaps she was right. His past reputation hadn't been very good, and, interestingly, before he came here with Star, there had never been any problems on the ranch.

Carlotta sighed.

She would have to watch the boy more closely, and also Lena and Cathy. But no matter who had betrayed her, she would ban them forever from Mercy Ranch, even if it turned out to be Cathy, whom she had grown to love long ago.

* * *

Hal and Cathy walked across the yard together. When they got to Carlotta's car, Cathy stopped abruptly and turned to Hal.

"Darn it! Yesterday I cried my eyes out, but today I'm furious with Carlotta. How can she think that it was me?" Angrily she kicked one of the tires, as though that could lessen her resentment.

"Hey, hey, hey! Come on, try to put yourself in Carlotta's shoes."

Cathy sighed. "I know you're right, but between Carlotta's mistrust and Lena's nastiness, I feel like a stray dog that's always getting kicked."

"Oh, Lena ... "

Cathy peered straight into Hal's eyes.

"Kevin told me that you said you still like me. Does that mean that you've broken up with Lena?"

The boy blushed. "Not yet, but ..."

"Oh, that's just terrific! Then just leave me alone!"
Cathy turned on her heels and ran back into the stable, past

Lena, who, not surprisingly, was still standing in the same spot outside the stable door. She never let Hal out of her sight for a minute.

"Can't you leave him alone?" she yelled at Cathy, but the girl just ignored her and kept going.

"You can kiss my feet!" Cathy shot back, and then disappeared into the tack room.

"I'd love to, if that would make you happy!"

"Who's making whom happy?" Beth and Logan, hand in hand, came walking in, and Lena smiled at them innocently.

"You two are just the ones to answer that question! Look in the mirror, and then you'll know!"

"What's up with her today? I've never seen her that friendly," commented Beth, a few minutes later. But before she could add anything else, her expression darkened. Ricki and Kevin had just arrived.

"Come on, let's go," she urged Logan, grabbing his arm and pulling him along for a few yards.

"Hey, what are you doing? Are you still having trouble with Ricki? Is she still acting strange?" asked Logan, and Beth shook her head.

"What happened this time?"

"Nothing," Beth didn't intend to tell her boyfriend about Ricki's vague suspicions, so she quickly changed the subject to something much less important.

* * *

When Dr. Hofer had finished vaccinating all the horses at Mercy Ranch, Carlotta accompanied him to his car, chatting easily with him, and then thanking him before saying good-bye. She watched him drive off and reflected on how lucky she was to have him as her vet. He, who had always led a life devoted to the wellbeing of animals, gave her a special price for her four-legged veterans, no matter what kind of treatment was involved.

"A mercy ranch has to be supported," he had said. "After all, the animals can't help it that their medicines are so expensive."

A smile spread over Carlotta's face. The world would be a better place if there were more people like Dr. Hofer.

She turned to walk back to the house. It was strangely quiet at the ranch today, although there were many young people around. Apparently they were all in the stable with the horses.

For a moment, Carlotta closed her eyes and enjoyed the quiet. She took a deep breath, and when she opened her eyes again, her glance fell on her car. It was leaning at a strange angle in front of the house.

"What happened here?" murmured Carlotta, frowning. "A flat tire? That's impossible!" Using her crutch to support her, she walked as quickly as she could to her car and bent down to inspect the tire.

This must be a bad joke, she thought. Then she stood up and shouted, "Heeey! Everybody come out here! And I mean *everybody*!"

"What's wrong now?" Lillian jumped at Carlotta's voice, which didn't sound at all like her. She looked at the others, but they all were in the dark as well.

When the kids joined the Mercy Ranch owner, she just pointed to her broken tire wordlessly.

"Who did that?" she asked, in a tone that demanded an answer, but all she got was a timid shaking of heads.

96

"I want to know who did it!"

Lena looked at Cathy as though she were asking for her forgiveness.

"Well, I heard that Cathy is furious with you and ... and I saw her kick your tires."

Hal spun around and confronted Lena.

"Stop it, Lena! That's ridiculous! Isn't it strange that you always see something that could look bad for Cathy?"

"I saw it, too," reported Bev, and nodded to Lena.

Carlotta folded her arms.

"A tire doesn't go flat when you kick it!" she responded firmly, but she couldn't help looking straight at Cathy. "It was slit!" Then her glance wandered to Logan. Hadn't Nick Rizzo called her up and warned her about the boy, who had supposedly also slit the tires of Avalon's chairman of the board?

Deep down, Carlotta now tended to believe that Logan was behind all of this, but no matter how much she thought about it, she couldn't come up with a reason why he should act like that at her ranch. And Cathy? She would never have thought that the girl could do something like that. She wasn't the type to destroy anything.

Cathy was breathless.

"Yeah, I was furious," she admitted sheepishly, "because I'm being labeled a thief, even though I'm not guilty. And it's true that I was so mad that I kicked the tire, but, Carlotta, you can't really believe that I ..."

Carlotta looked over the kids' heads into the distance.

"I don't know what I should think any more. I'd like all of you to go home now! Perhaps you could all think about what's happening here. And think about whether it's okay. Good-bye!" she said firmly, and then marched back and disappeared into the house without another word.

Each and every one of the young people stood around looking stunned and dejected. It was the first time they had ever seen Carlotta that angry, and they understood the reason for it. But still, to send them home?

In each of them, mistrust began to grow, and as much as they fought against it – especially Ricki, Lillian, and Kevin – they couldn't stop themselves from glancing at Cathy and Logan out of the corners of their eyes.

"Come on, let's saddle our horses and ride home," said Lillian finally. And so with bowed heads and heavy steps, they all went back to the stable.

"Thanks," Cathy was just able to say, weakly, as she went past Hal.

"Hal, are you coming?" Lena shrilly called out at the same moment.

"No!" shouted Hal, really ticked off.

Strangely, this time Lena accepted his answer without comment. Apparently indifferent, she took her friend Bev's arm and walked over to their bikes, ready to go home as well.

Logan, however, was still standing beside Beth in front of the car, as if he had been struck by lightning. He was still staring at the door to the ranch house, behind which Carlotta had just disappeared.

"Logan?" Beth softly called to her boyfriend and tugged gently at his sleeve, but he shook off her touch, fuming with anger.

"Leave me alone!"

"But ..."

He pointed at the door. "She thinks it was me!"

"Nonsense."

"Didn't you see the look in her eyes? I felt it! For her, I'm the bad guy!" His face turned stonier as Beth watched helplessly. "I bet she talked with Rizzo, so there's nothing else to say. Logan was a bad guy in New York, then he messed up the private riding stables, and slit the tires of the Board chairman's car... What could be more logical than continuing my urge to slice tires here? The only thing she's hasn't blamed me for yet is the missing money!" he said bitterly.

Then he turned around abruptly and ran to his bike without even looking to see if Beth was following him. In his heart he began to feel a growing anger toward Carlotta, who, he suspected, wasn't as unprejudiced toward him as Beth had claimed. How could he have believed that Carlotta would be willing to give him a chance? She was just like all the others. If something happened somewhere, he was always to blame. That's the way it had always been, and apparently that's the way it was going to stay.

Similar thoughts were going through Cathy's mind as she rode home in deep silence with her three friends. None of them felt like expressing his or her thoughts.

Sadly, the girl sensed that her friends, just like Carlotta, couldn't decide whether Cathy had something to do with all this, but Cathy promised herself one thing: she would not go back to Mercy Ranch until the real culprit was found, even if the others might think that she was staying away because of a guilty conscience.

* * *

"Now I really don't know what to believe," Lillian admitted freely, as she sat in the stable that evening with Ricki and Kevin after Cathy had left for home. "On one hand, Cathy, on the other, Logan. As dumb as it sounds, everything makes each one look guilty. I'm so glad I'm not a detective and have to deal with these kinds of cases every day. It doesn't seem so easy to find the real guilty person."

"That's true. But tell me, honestly, do you think Cathy is capable of stealing money and slicing tires?" asked Ricki.

"Not really."

"Your favorite culprit is still Logan, isn't it?" Kevin looked at his girlfriend closely.

Ricki shrugged her shoulders.

"I'm sorry, but yes, I think he's behind all this. I know Cathy couldn't do it!"

Kevin didn't say anything more for a while, but then he spoke softly, "I'm beginning to think you're right. It could have been him."

"And if not?" Lillian leaned against the wall of Holli's stall and stroked his mane absently.

Kevin stood up. "There is one way of finding out. We'll have to spend as much time as possible at Mercy Ranch tomorrow and the next few days. If it really was Logan, he'll betray himself sooner or later, or maybe he'll do some other damage. If we're lucky, we'll catch him in the act."

"Unless Carlotta throws us off the ranch right from the start," Ricki added.

"She won't do that. We're not suspects!" commented

100

Lillian. "She was just sick and tired of all of us today, which isn't surprising, is it?"

Ricki nodded.

"All right, then, let's do something to prove Cathy's innocence!" she suggested.

"Or Logan's," added Kevin, and Ricki didn't contradict him, even though she wanted to.

* * *

Beth couldn't sleep at all that night. She turned back and forth restlessly, thinking about Logan and about what he had said. It still hurt her that he had left her standing there and had gone home without saying good-bye.

She wondered if over the last few weeks she had been unfair to Ricki for judging her because of what she thought of Logan.

Beth pulled her pillow over her head and tried to push the conflicting thoughts out of her mind.

Chapter 7

In the following days Cathy rode Rashid alone through the countryside, although sometimes the gelding spent peaceful days on the paddock with Salina and Chico, his pony mare and donkey stable mates, because Cathy's problems weighed so heavily on her mind that she didn't even feel like riding.

On the other hand, Ricki, Kevin, and Lillian rode over to Mercy Ranch every day, as they had discussed, and were always greeted warmly by Carlotta; however, it was obvious that Carlotta's usual enthusiasm at seeing them was turned down to a low flame. With a disappointing sadness, she had noticed that Cathy stayed away from the ranch and, just as the girl had thought, Carlotta interpreted this as a confession of guilt.

"I guess I misjudged her after all," was the bitter conclusion she drew after a week. Carlotta was almost ready to apologize to Logan for her seeming incorrect misgivings about him, but something held her back, something she couldn't explain even to herself.

Between Beth and her boyfriend there was also a tense, almost frosty atmosphere, because Logan had retreated from almost everything and everyone. He couldn't even bear to be near Beth. He sensed that she, too, had doubts and was no longer behind him one hundred percent. This was one more bitter experience that upset him. As a result, he gave one-syllable answers when she asked him anything, and he rode off on Star every day so that he could think everything over. But rather than help him, his isolation caused him to become somewhat aggressive.

Deeply hurt by his behavior, Beth turned again to her friends, and even complained about her problems to Ricki.

"I hardly recognize him any more," she said, disappointed. "He's changed so much ever since that incident with Carlotta's car."

Ricki put her arms around her friend.

"Come on, don't worry about it. That's just the way he is," she said, but at the same time the voice in her head added, *and he's worse than I thought if he's now pushing Beth away like this*.

"Let's go for a nice ride – that'll make you feel better," she suggested, and Beth nodded, wiping a tear from her eye.

"May I join you?" asked Hal, who also was moping around, because Cathy no longer came to the ranch.

"Of course!" Kevin smiled, giving him a pat on the shoulder. "Jonah will whinny a cheer if he gets to cool off his soft old bones at Echo Lake."

And so the kids got ready to leave, hoping they could

shake off their depressing thoughts on a wonderful ride in the beautiful weather.

Through the window Carlotta watched them ride away before sinking down heavily into her office chair. She dearly wished that peace and well-being would return to her ranch and that the mystery of the missing envelopes would soon be resolved. The real culprit still had not been discovered, and Carlotta hoped that whoever it was would come to her voluntarily and confess everything. It wasn't in her nature to accuse anyone because of some doubtful observations.

Carlotta decided to give the culprit one more week. If he or she didn't own up to the thievery by then, she would have no choice but to call Cathy and Logan into her office for a serious talk.

* * *

Logan rode through the woods with no real destination. He was tense, furious, sad – a fireworks of emotions that raged within him and inevitably were picked up by Star.

Nervous, the Arabian held his head high, his nostrils extended, and pranced forward with short steps. Logan, who usually rode his horse with loose reins, had to hold them tightly otherwise Star would have bolted.

"What's going on?" he yelled at his horse from the saddle, as he kept giving him the familiar signals, but instead of holding back, the horse got more fidgety.

Star began to jerk his head moodily and blow his unhappiness out through his nostrils with a hissing noise.

"You're really getting on my nerves today!" snarled Logan, equally angry, but he knew that the animal's behavior just mirrored his own.

He sighed.

Logan loved his horse more than anything in the world and he had never had any problems with him. The sensitivity with which Star had always reacted to Logan's feelings usually caused the boy to get himself under control and to calm down, but today Star's behavior was having just the opposite effect.

Logan's tension grew with every dancing step the animal took, and soon he was convinced it would have been better if he hadn't gotten into the saddle today.

Then Logan remembered something he once read:

Gaze into the eyes of your horse
and you will recognize the mirror of your soul.

Pay attention to the behavior of your horse,
and you will see how you appear to others.

Only mount your horse when you are happy,
otherwise you will have a fight with yourself,
which, considering the strength of the animal,
you will inevitably lose.

"Whoever said that sure had it right," murmured Logan, the meaning of the words sinking in. At the same moment, Star pulled the reins out of his hands and bolted forward at an incredible speed, or so it seemed to his rider, whose unspoken wish was to flee from the things that were making his life difficult.

Star's fast gallop caught Logan by surprise and at first

he had enormous difficulty staying in the saddle. But since he was a good rider, he finally managed to adapt himself to the rhythm of his horse and find his balance again.

He automatically grabbed onto Star's mane, and bent way over the animal's neck, trying to grab the reins that had slipped out of his sweaty hands and slid up toward the horse's ears. He almost had the leather in his hands when Star jumped like a rabbit and sped deeper into the woods.

"Star, are you crazy?" yelled Logan at his horse. "Stand still, Star! Whoa!" But the white Arabian just seemed to go faster, springing over tree trunks and roots on the ground and ignoring his rider, who was concentrating on not falling out of the saddle.

* * *

Cathy paced back and forth in her room. She tried to read but she couldn't focus on a single sentence. After school she had called Ricki's number a few times, and Lillian's as well, but she couldn't reach either one, and they probably couldn't have helped her anyway.

Sighing, she remembered that she still had homework to do, so she opened her books and notebooks listlessly, although she already knew she wouldn't be able to concentrate. She could still see Carlotta's questioning and disappointed look.

"If I only knew what to do!" Cathy thought desperately. She thought about telling her mother about her problems, but decided against it. Her mother was never objective, which made conversations like this more difficult. Anyway, it always seemed easier to talk about her problems with people outside the family. But who else could Cathy call?

There had to be someone she could talk to, someone who could give her some good advice.

She wondered if she should talk to Jake about what had happened. But no, she decided that wouldn't work. After all, she knew the old man had heart trouble, and this kind of conversation might upset him too much.

Cathy went to the window and looked outside. There was only one possibility that would give her any peace. She had to go directly into the lion's den. She had to go to Carlotta.

* * *

After a beautiful, relaxed gallop, the young folks let their horses walk on loose reins.

"I'm so thirsty, I could drink the whole lake," groaned Ricki and looked longingly at Echo Lake, which had just come into view. "It's really muggy today!"

"I feel the same way," responded Kevin, mopping his forehead and neck with his shirtsleeve. "When we get back to the stable, I'm going to charge the next available trough!"

"Sharazan won't like that," laughed Lillian, as she imagined Kevin trying to work the mechanism on the trough with his tongue.

"I'm actually considering jumping into the water with all my clothes on," Ricki continued.

"I wonder if Logan will ever be normal again?" asked Beth, out of the blue.

"Oh, no ... not again!" Kevin sagged dramatically in the saddle. "Didn't we agree not to talk about our problems on this ride?"

"I'm sorry, but I can't think of anything else," apologized Beth.

107

"I know what you mean," Hal looked glumly at Beth. "We can't just ignore certain topics. All I think about is Cathy! I wonder how she is right now."

"Probably just as unhappy as Logan!"

"Man! Maybe it would be better if *you two* dove into Echo Lake to clear your heads."

Ricki grimaced, but she had to admit that she, too, had been having the same thoughts for the past two hours.

"Can't we just turn around and ride back to the ranch? Maybe he's already back." Beth glanced pleadingly at her friends.

"I don't feel like riding anymore either," agreed Hal.

"Well, it's too humid for me, too, so as far as I'm concerned, we can ride back," replied Lillian.

"All agreed," Kevin nodded. "Let's go!"

"Okay!" four out of the five said in unison.

"Oh, c'mon, you guys! Here we are, so close to the lake, and you want to go back," Ricki pouted. She loved Echo Lake, which lay idyllically in the middle of the woods. "All right, ride back. I'm going to go down to the water, and then I'll follow you."

"Okay, see you later."

While Lillian and company started the ride back, Ricki steered Diablo in a lazy trot toward the lake. She knew the entire shoreline by heart, hidden behind tall bushes and almost never crowded with swimmers, so at some point she dismounted and led Diablo through the dense undergrowth down to the edge of the lake and allowed the beauty of nature to work its magic on her.

Every time she came here with her horse, she felt

a calmness and an incredible happiness she never felt anywhere else. She leaned against Diablo's neck dreamily, and as she regarded the surface of the water with all of its shimmering colors, she wasn't upset that the others hadn't come with her.

How beautiful it was here!

She enjoyed the undisturbed closeness to her beloved black horse and the feeling that she and Diablo were all alone in the world. Suddenly she felt like the richest person in the world.

"You like it here, too, don't you?" she asked Diablo softly. He was rubbing his forehead lovingly against her, but when he began to sling his tail in a circle Ricki tore herself away from the wonderful view in front of her and led her horse back to the path. The bloodthirsty horseflies now storming Diablo's sweaty coat were particularly stubborn, and Ricki was glad to be back in the woods and away from the lake.

Although her clothes were damp from the heat, Ricki didn't want to ride home yet, so she decided to take a little detour before following her friends.

* * *

Lena was astonished when Cathy arrived at Mercy Ranch on Rashid. She hadn't thought the girl would dare show up there after the tire incident.

"What are you doing here? You're not welcome here, or haven't you noticed?" she sniped at her adversary.

"Get out of my way!" Cathy jumped down from the saddle and started to lead Rashid into the stable.

"Don't even think about it! Just ride back where you came from and don't let me catch you here ever again! Or ... "

109

"Or …?" Cathy challenged.

Lena smiled evilly, but she didn't answer. Mumbling softly to herself, she jumped out of the way as Cathy continued toward the stable with Rashid, with no regard for Lena's toes.

"You just wait!" Lena turned and left in a rage.

Cathy sighed with relief. She wasn't nearly as confident as she had appeared. On the contrary! She felt sick to her stomach. She dreaded the talk with Carlotta.

Slowly she unsaddled Rashid and rethought yet again what she intended to say to the older woman.

"Why is this so tough?" she asked Rashid, as she buried her face in his mane. She snuggled up against him to gather some strength for what was awaiting her. Then, summoning her courage, she left the stall and entered the house through the connecting door to Carlotta's living quarters.

Taking a deep breath, she called, "Carlotta? Carlotta! Are you home?"

The office door opened.

"Cathy ... you came," Carlotta said softly, as her heart cramped painfully in her chest.

"I ... I have to talk to you. If I don't, I'll go crazy!" Cathy swallowed hard.

* * *

Star raced back and forth through the narrowly spaced trees without slowing down. Logan was hunched like a monkey over the back of his horse, unable to stop him.

Suddenly, the horse started another jump over a tree stump, but at the last moment he sensed that the jump would fail and tried to stop. However, Star couldn't prevent

110

himself from landing in a ditch covered with undergrowth, and there he remained, fallen down, dazed.

Logan had been thrown out of the saddle in a high arc, and he too lay still for a few moments, until he came to and started to move his limbs carefully. Still a little unsure of himself, he staggered to his feet and looked at his horse in shock.

"Star? Star!" he shouted at him, at first softly and then loudly, fearful that his horse was injured.

The white horse raised his head as if to say, Don't worry, nothing happened! But he didn't try to get up.

Logan slid quickly down the embankment and kneeled beside his horse.

"What a silly thing to do, you dummy!" he said, his voice trembling. "Did you have to race through the woods like a lunatic? Come on, get up!"

The boy grabbed the reins and tried to get his horse to stand, but beyond a few strained attempts to get his legs positioned correctly, Star couldn't make it. He was lying too awkwardly in the narrow ditch, his legs pointing upward, and his hooves couldn't find any hold that would allow him to push himself up and stand.

After a few attempts, the horse gave up, and Logan was close to panic.

"Star! What am I going to do with you?" Exhausted, he sat down in the dirt while he stroked Star's head. "You *have to* stand up! Oh, if I wish I knew how to help you!"

Hopelessly, he looked around and tried to concentrate, but his fear for the Arabian overwhelmed him and prevented him from thinking clearly.

He stood up again and tried to get his horse to do the

same, but although Star's neck got longer when he pulled on the reins, the horse didn't move.

Logan's panic grew. What could he do? He couldn't leave his horse alone and run back to the ranch to get help, and there were none of the usual hikers walking the trails around Echo Lake. To make matters worse, Star's right hind ankle was beginning to swell, and it was clear to Logan that the longer he waited the more difficult it would be for Star to get up.

His eyes flew wildly back and forth, looking for something or someone to help. Suddenly he spied a hazelnut bush. He stood up quickly, climbed out of the ditch, ran over to the bush and, with some effort, broke off a long branch.

As he ran back to Star, he removed the leaves from the hazelnut branch. Then he placed himself hesitantly behind his horse. If Star didn't get up voluntarily, he would have to force him, even if it meant using this temporary whip, which would break Logan's heart. For his entire life as a rider, he had been strongly against using a rider's whip, but now he would have to shock Star so much that the animal would do anything to turn himself around and get up.

Hastily Logan took a few breaths with his eyes closed. Then he raised his arm and brought it down hard, beating his beloved horse across the croup with the branch and yelling at him as loudly as he could.

"Get up, Star! You have to GET UP! Stand up! STAND UP! Come on, come on, come on! UP!" He screamed like a madman as the hazelnut branch swept down.

Logan would never forget the frightened wide eyes

of his horse and the numerous failed attempts until, with wild efforts, Star finally managed to get up onto his legs. Stumbling and slipping, he climbed out of the ditch and afterward, completely drenched with sweat, eyes rolling, nostrils extended, trembling, he stood still.

Logan dropped the branch and immediately stood beside Star to calm him down. He held the reins tightly in his hand as he petted his horse and spoke quietly to him.

At that moment he couldn't have expressed how glad he was that his horse was standing in front of him again, but at the same time, he felt just awful.

"You know I had to do it, don't you, Star? Please forgive me!" he whispered to his best friend.

* * *

Cathy sat hunched over on the chair in front of Carlotta's desk and kneaded her fingers nervously. Once again, she asked herself why she was so nervous. After all, she hadn't done anything.

"It's good that you found your way here," Carlotta finally broke the silence. "I'm glad that you came." Then she paused a moment. "Cathy ... you know me well by now, and you know that you can tell me anything."

The girl nodded.

"I just keep asking myself why you waited so long to talk to me about your problems," Carlotta continued. "If you needed money for something, then you could have asked me, without ... "

Cathy's head flew up and, like before, she stared at Carlotta in disbelief.

"No, no! For heaven's sake!" she stammered, shaking her

head as though hypnotized. "Carlotta, you don't understand ... I didn't come here to tell you that I'm guilty of anything!"

"No? Then why?" came the bewildered question.

"I just can't stand it anymore that everyone thinks I'm a thief! Carlotta, I swear by everything I hold dear – on Rashid's life, on the life of my parents, I swear that I didn't do it! And I didn't have anything to do with the tires either. Please, Carlotta, please, you have to believe me. I didn't steal anything and I didn't slit your tires. If I'm lying, let me fall over dead!" Cathy's eyes filled with tears.

Carlotta remained silent as she studied the girl whom she'd always felt a special fondness for, and tried to decide whether or not she was telling the truth.

"And why should I believe you when so much speaks against you?" she asked at last.

Cathy looked at her desperately, the tears now wetting her cheeks.

"Because ... because you know me ... You know that I would never do such a thing," she managed to say as she looked directly at Carlotta.

The older woman held Cathy's gaze as she leaned in to her.

"So it wasn't you?"

"No!"

"Then who was it?"

Cathy's heart raced wildly.

"I don't know! Really! I could say the name of anyone who goes in and out of Mercy Ranch now, but that wouldn't be fair, because I just don't know!"

Carlotta nodded and stood up straight. Then she gestured for Cathy to come closer.

She stood up, her knees shaking, and walked around the desk. Carlotta wrapped her arms around her.

"It really wasn't you. If you had been guilty you would have tried to put the blame on someone else, and you didn't do that. But apart from that, I would have been very surprised if it had been you," she said softly, as she stroked the girl's hair.

"Now calm down. It's okay. Everything's okay."

Now Cathy really began to cry, but this time it was tears of relief not despair.

"I'm ... I'm so glad you believe me!" she stammered. "I couldn't have stood it another day."

"Me neither," smiled Carlotta. "Okay, now. How about we go over to my kitchen and make ourselves a snack? I could use a cup of coffee!"

"I'd like a soda," sniffed Cathy, as she let herself be guided out the door.

"Fine. Afterward, the world will look a lot better!"

Cathy nodded vigorously.

"It already does, Carlotta! Honestly!"

* * *

"What's keeping Ricki?" Lillian looked around once again. "Didn't she say she was going to follow us?"

"You know Ricki. When she's at Echo Lake she forgets the time," replied Kevin. "It could be quite a while before she gets here."

"Maybe she rode straight home," Beth suggested, but Kevin was sure she hadn't.

"No, I doubt it. If she said she was going to come with us, then she will ... But as strange as she's been these last few weeks, it isn't completely out of the question that she –"

"Hang it up, Kevin! She was fine today, and yesterday, too. I think her weirdness is over." Lillian grinned.

"You mean, because she kept saying things against Logan it almost ruined her friendship with you guys?" Beth glanced sideways at a rabbit that was rapidly running away as the horses came near him.

"What else?"

Beth shrugged her shoulders.

"Maybe ... maybe she wasn't that far off."

"What?" Lillian brought Holli to a stop and stared at her friend. "I can't believe you just said that!"

"And it still isn't clear whether Cathy was behind the whole thing," added Kevin.

"Cathy didn't have anything to do with it," announced Hal with conviction.

"Listen, Hal, I'm not saying anything either way, believe me. I just said that in theory."

"Well then, stop saying it! It wasn't Cathy and that's all there is to it!"

Kevin puffed out his cheeks and exhaled noisily.

"Fine! Now let's think this thing over carefully, okay? And without anyone thinking that he or she has to defend someone. Is that clear?"

The others looked at him quizzically, not quite understanding what Kevin meant.

"All right. Let's suppose it wasn't Cathy," he began to explain. "And let's suppose it wasn't Logan, either."

"Yeah, and…?"

"Well, who was it then? Who else could it be?"

"Oh, if only it were that easy!"

"Hmmm ... if everyone keeps their mouths shut, then we're never going to find out who's having a good time at Carlotta's expense."

"That's true. So let's hope for a miracle."

"It looks like we'll need one."

Chapter 8

Ricki was thinking about how many weeks of school were left before summer vacation when she heard terrible shouting. Although she wasn't able to understand a single word, she rode into the woods, a little scared but nevertheless curious. She kept looking around until finally she spied a person in the distance, waving his arms wildly.

"Oh, no! Something bad must have happened," she said to her horse, and steered Diablo in that direction.

When she got closer, her heart almost stopped beating as she recognized Logan, who was yelling and hitting something with what looked like a tree branch. But she couldn't yet tell who or what he was beating. It was only when she saw Star get up from the ditch with great effort that everything become clear.

"That miserable rat!" Ricki, in a fury, urged Diablo forward, but was very careful to keep him from stepping on the roots that were barely visible under the moss.

A few yards in front of Logan she brought Diablo to a halt.

"You are the worst kind of person in the world, Logan Bendix! Really, the worst!" Ricki could hardly keep her voice under control.

The boy, who was standing beside his horse when he heard her, looked around in confusion.

"What?"

"You are a horrible, disgusting monster! You're cruel to animals! You beat your horse until he was lying on the ground!"

"I didn't beat Star!"

"Of course you did! I saw you!" Ricki became more enraged by the moment.

"You got it all wrong."

"Hah! As if there was anything to get wrong! It's not right, beating that poor horse like that! Look at him, he's still trembling all over."

Logan shook his head. He knew that as long as Ricki believed what she saw was the truth, he wouldn't be able to convince her of what really had happened.

"Come on, Star, let's go," he said softly to his white horse and pulled gently on the reins.

Slowly, the animal began to limp forward.

"What did you do to him? He can't even walk. I was right! You're awful!"

"Would you please stop? You don't understand anything. How could you? You don't know what happened!" Logan was upset now, too, but Ricki wasn't so easy to get rid of.

"I understand perfectly! I saw you beating him. Do you hear me? I SAW YOU!"

119

Logan rolled his eyes. "You're just like Lena! She always says she saw something, and I doubt she did!" he said angrily.

"What do you mean by that?" asked Ricki, watching him carefully.

"Nothing!"

"If you doubt what Lena said, then you must know more about the whole thing. Maybe it *was* you who took the envelope with the money and slit the tires."

Logan whirled around.

"Now you listen, you witch! Be careful what you say, or you might get a bad reputation yourself for spreading lies! Do you hear me? Now, leave me alone!" Logan's fury was really out of control. Who did this uppity girl think she was?

"Don't worry, I'm out of here. But you can be sure that this thing with Star is going to have consequences for you, Logan Bendix! People who are cruel to animals don't get away with it around here!"

With those words Ricki turned Diablo around and, looking back at Logan with scorn, she rode out of the woods.

But Ricki couldn't calm down. She kept picturing Logan shouting and beating Star with his stick and, afterward, the horse, lame, completely filthy, covered in sweat, and trembling.

"Carlotta is going to kill him!" she said to Diablo, and as soon as he was back on the firm path through the woods, she allowed him to break into a light canter.

The idea of a longer ride was forgotten. Now all she wanted was to ride back to the ranch as fast as possible so that she could tell Carlotta immediately about the incident she just witnessed.

The closer Ricki came to the ranch, the more she was convinced that Logan was to blame for everything that had happened there. And the more certain she became, the more aware she was that she didn't enjoy being right about her classmate.

No! He's not worth wasting even one thought on! she told herself, and let up on the reins a little when she reached a long stretch of meadow.

"Run, Diablo!" she called. "Run, my boy! We have to get home. Who knows what else that guy is going to do to his horse?" And as if there were a psychic connection between the black horse and his owner, Diablo stretched his muscular body and raced over the meadow, his hooves barely touching the ground.

* * *

"Hey, it doesn't look as though Ricki fell asleep at the lake after all," grinned Kevin, pointing behind them. "There she is, back there ... and look at her go!"

Lillian turned around to look.

"Something's wrong! She wouldn't let Diablo gallop through the countryside in this heat unless something happened!"

Together the friends waited until Ricki stopped her horse beside them.

"Hey, are you being chased by the devil?" teased Kevin, but when he saw Ricki's face he knew that whatever had happened was not a joking matter.

"The devil has many faces," Ricki answered, out of breath. "Come on, let's keep going. I have to get to Carlotta."

"Wait a sec. Tell us, what happened!"

"I saw Logan."

"Oh, no, did something happen to him?" Beth turned as pale as a ghost.

"No! He's doing too well, I'm sorry to say! But Star ... Logan beat him pretty badly. I saw him!"

"What?"

"That's impossible!"

"No, really?"

The friends looked at each other, not knowing what to believe.

"You're kidding!"

"Do I look like I am?"

"Are you sure it was Logan? I mean, isn't it possible that –" Beth felt everything turn upside down inside her. She would have believed some things about Logan, but she couldn't possibly imagine that he would beat Star. He loved that horse!

"Of course I'm sure! I'm not an idiot! We talked and he denied it, but I saw him."

"You sound like Lena."

"Oh, man! That's what HE said!" Ricki was very anxious to get back to the ranch. "Can't we ride a little faster?"

Lillian pointed at Diablo, whose coat glistened with sweat.

"It's too hot for a fast gallop. Look at Diablo. I think he wants to go a little more slowly."

"I know, I know, but I'm so upset. I hope he doesn't hit him again."

"Calm down, Ricki. Do you really believe that Logan

is going to hit his horse on the way home? That's crazy, don't you think?" Hal, like Beth, wasn't willing to believe Ricki's description of the horror show.

"You can think what you want," Ricki replied. She forced herself to trot beside the others, but when Mercy Ranch came into view nothing could stop her. She urged her horse into a full gallop and hoped that Carlotta was at home.

* * *

Cathy and Carlotta were just leaving the stable, laughing happily and followed by a grim Lena, who couldn't understand why the two of them were best friends again.

With surprised expressions, they watched Ricki approach. She had left the group of riders and come galloping hard toward them.

She had hardly reached the ranch house when she sprang down from the saddle and reported hastily what she had seen, while the three others listened attentively.

Carlotta's face was all seriousness as she listened to Ricki, and when the girl finished, the ranch owner pointed to the stable.

"First bring Diablo inside. He's completely drenched in sweat!"

"And what's going to happen to Logan?"

"You said that Star was limping so I'm going to drive to them with the horse trailer. At least that old thing that Dr. Hofer left here last month will be put to use for once." Carlotta waved to Cathy to come with her.

"I'll drive in reverse toward the trailer and you can hook it on, okay?"

Cathy nodded and ran behind the stable where the trailer

was standing. Less than three minutes later, Carlotta's car rolled toward her.

"It'd be best if you come with me. Who knows if we'll have difficulty loading the horse onto the trailer, and if we do it's always better to have one more person to help."

"Okay," Cathy said. She got in quickly and off they went.

While they were on the way, the girl asked herself if Carlotta was thinking the same thing she was. After all, according to Ricki, it seemed that Logan had practically admitted his guilt by what he said. However, Carlotta was silent. Of course she was thinking about Logan too, but she was one hundred percent sure that in spite of all the things he may have done at the ranch, he would never mishandle his horse. She would swear to that if necessary.

Sometimes I do make mistakes in my judgment, but I know enough about riding and horses to know that Logan loves his Star more than anything, she thought.

"Back there! He's back there!" Cathy pointed excitedly across the meadow, to the path at the edge of the woods, to where Logan was walking very slowly with Star.

Carlotta slowed down with a screech and then drove on cautiously. She didn't want to miss the entrance to the path that led to the boy.

* * *

Logan had stopped his horse and was now staring dismally at the vehicle slowly coming toward him, bouncing over the stones. It came to a stop a few feet from him.

Carlotta got out awkwardly. Her leg, which had been injured in a riding accident many years earlier, was particularly painful in the humid weather, and she leaned on the crutch that always accompanied her.

"What happened to Star?" she asked calmly, looking kindly at Logan. Cathy was surprised at Carlotta's unemotional reaction. "Ricki said something was wrong with him, and I thought it would be better to transport him back to the ranch in the trailer."

"He's limping," Logan answered brusquely. He was sure that Ricki had told Carlotta her fairy tale.

"And why?"

"Because he bolted and raced through the woods."

"Oh! That can happen." Carlotta waited for Logan to explain further, but he didn't intend to.

Why should I? Logan thought. *She won't believe me anyway! No one does!*

The boy felt bitter as he stared at the woman.

"Okay, then take Star's saddle off," said Carlotta, finally. "Cathy, please open the loading ramp. It's time to go home." And turning to Logan, she asked, "Will Star go into the trailer easily?"

The boy nodded.

"Good, then let's go." She stepped aside and Logan led his horse past her. Carlotta glanced at Star's croup and saw a few marks on his coat, but knew that low-hanging branches could have caused them.

The horse allowed them to lead him into the trailer without any objections, and after Logan had put Star's saddle in the trunk of the car, Carlotta drove slowly back to the ranch without anyone saying another word.

* * *

125

As Logan got out of the car to unload Star at Mercy Ranch, almost all of the people who gathered to meet the trailer looked as if they were against him. Only Beth gazed at him with a mixture of sadness and uncertainty. When he walked past her, he knew that she was waiting for an explanation about what had really happened, but he also sensed that she no longer believed in him completely.

Logan felt very disappointed at that, and his anger at Ricki began to grow. "Thanks a lot!" he hissed at her, before slowly leading his horse into the stable.

Ricki's face reddened against her will. She had to admit that at the moment she didn't feel very comfortable with the situation, but then everything she saw came back to her again, so she just clenched her teeth. If there was anything that she couldn't forgive, it was hurting an animal. In such instances, Ricki was immovable.

Carlotta had gone into the tack room and when she returned she went to Star's stall with a jar of salve.

"Here," she said to Logan. "Rub his ankle with this twice a day and then put a bandage on it. This stuff is really good, and I think he'll be fine in two or three days."

Logan nodded gratefully, but he avoided looking into Carlotta's piercing eyes. When Beth appeared suddenly, and Carlotta disappeared, he felt a lot better.

Beth looked at her boyfriend for a long while, silent, and then she asked softly, "Is it true?"

"Is what true?"

"That you ... that you hit Star?"

Logan knelt down beside his horse and began to rub the salve in without another word.

126

Beth waited a long time for an answer and when one didn't come, she turned away.

"Your silence says everything. So Ricki was right! Logan, how could you? I would never have believed that of you! Never! I ... I don't want anything to do with you ever again! NEVER! Do you understand?"

With a sob, the girl ran out of the stable. She could hardly believe what she had just said. After all, she liked Logan so much! But what he had done was just too awful.

Logan winced at her words, but he said nothing. There was just no point.

* * *

A few days passed, days in which Logan felt like an outcast both at school and at the Ranch. At least Star had healed, and he began to exercise him slowly.

Beth avoided Logan as much as possible, but in spite of everything that had happened, she regretted her angry words and missed Logan a lot.

Carlotta, on the other hand, had waited for him to say something about Star, but it didn't look as though Logan was going to volunteer anything about what had actually happened in the woods. She had said nothing about the money or the tires.

"I don't understand Carlotta," Ricki said more than once. "Since when doesn't she get outraged when someone is cruel to a horse? Honestly, I'm really disappointed! I could have sworn that she would have given Logan a real talking to by now."

"She must have her reasons," Lillian tried to placate her friend.

"If you could tell me just one, I would really appreciate it! Maybe I could understand it ... Hey, what's going on with those two over there?" Ricki pointed to the small outdoor riding ring, where Cathy and Hal were talking, waving their arms around wildly.

Kevin grinned.

"It looks as though Hal has finally managed to talk to Cathy. By the way, did you two know that he broke up with Lena yesterday?"

"No, really?"

"Yep!"

"Oh, now I know why Lena's been in such a horrible mood all day!" responded Lillian.

"Don't tell me that you would have been surprised anyway. She's always in a bad mood!"

Lena stood in the stable doorway, her eyes shooting imaginary daggers at Hal and Cathy. It was so humiliating for her to see the two of them together again. It didn't occur to her that not too long ago Cathy had felt exactly the same. Lena wished them all kinds of horrible things in her mind, and she swore to herself that she was going to make their lives miserable, even though she still didn't know how she was going to do it. Her glance traveled to the other riders, who were leaning their arms on the paddock fence, watching the horses graze and occasionally looking over at her.

You are all as ridiculous as they are! Lena thought angrily. *They're all idiots! And Carlotta – that old bat – thinks she's something special just because she has a few old horses on her ranch and is practically idolized by most of the kids.*

128

Lena's nasty thoughts were almost limitless, and when Carlotta came out of the house, the girl turned away in disgust and disappeared into the stable. She didn't feel like listening to any lame remarks such as, "You don't look good." "How are you?" "Can I help you?"

Why am I here, anyway? she asked herself, kicking up hay with the toe of her boot. *None of them likes me!* Then suddenly she hesitated. *Logan has become an outcast, too ... Hmmm ... maybe I could ... yeah, that's it!*

Lena put a phony smile on her face then turned around, and with an air of pretend friendliness, walked out into the yard to wait for Logan to return from his slow, short ride on Star. She was sure he would become her ally.

Logan saw the ranch in front of him. He could recognize Beth and her friends from a distance. Sweet Beth ... what a great time he had with her, and how wonderful the future could have been if not for that self-righteous Ricki. In four weeks the renovation of the Bendixes' stable would be completed, and Star would be able to move into his permanent home. It would have been so wonderful if Beth could have boarded Rondo there as well.

Logan sighed.

Beth, the only person besides his parents who had made him feel worthwhile and loved – had turned away from him because that know-it-all had wrongly interpreted what she had seen and then told everyone.

He mulled over why he hadn't told Beth or Carlotta the true story. But as he thought about it, he shook his head firmly, realizing it wouldn't have made any difference. No one would have believed him, of that he was still convinced. The thing that bothered him most, however, was the fact that Carlotta, who always stood up for mishandled animals, had never said anything to him. Not on the day she picked up Star with the trailer, and not afterward. That was really strange, and Logan didn't understand why.

At that moment he realized that he had never thanked her for coming to get Star so quickly and bringing him back to the ranch. Logan was really ashamed of himself for forgetting.

I can still do it! he thought, and decided he would apologize as soon as Star was comfortable in his stall or out on the paddock.

* * *

"Admit it. You can't stand them, either!" Lena said to Logan as he unsaddled his horse.

"And what if I can't?"

Lena smiled warmly.

"Well, I wouldn't let them call me an animal torturer and thief and –"

Logan whirled around.

"Would you please shut up and leave me alone? You're just mad that Hal broke up with you!"

"That, too, but that has nothing to do with –"

"Get lost!" Logan shouted, and bent down to busy himself cleaning the mud out Star's hooves.

Lena bit her lip.

"Cathy has gotten to Carlotta. That means they'll suspect you as the thief as well as the tire slasher, even though I saw Cathy do it, but nobody believes me." She paused briefly. "If she were caught in the act of doing something, then you would be home free."

"And? Am I supposed to go to her and say, 'Hey Cathy, why don't you slash Carlotta's other tire, but tell me before you do it, so that we can all watch,' or what? Admit it, Lena, you don't care whether they stop suspecting me; you just want something bad to happen to Cathy!"

Lena turned red.

"Well, maybe a little," she confessed and winked at Logan.

And maybe because she had owned up to her anger at Cathy, she had won a little admiration from the boy. Yeah, when he thought about it, it wasn't such a bad idea. They should plan something so that Cathy would fall into the trap, and then ...

"I'll think about it, but for now, leave me alone!" responded Logan. He nodded to Lena and led Star out of his stall and past her so that he could have an hour on the paddock.

Lena rubbed her hands together with glee as she watched him go. Logan was sly enough to think of something good that would hurt Cathy forever. And then ... yeah, then it would be Hal's turn! Lena was going to make sure he would regret breaking up with her!

* * *

Diablo, Sharazan, Rashid and Holli were also on Carlotta's paddock, waiting for the friends to be ready to ride back home. When Logan pushed the paddock bars aside so that he could let Star onto the meadow, Diablo moved forward, and Logan nudged him aside a little roughly.

"Don't you dare touch my horse!" called out Ricki and ran over to him.

131

"Calm down! I didn't do anything!" Logan looked at her contemptuously. "I'm only cruel to horses when I don't have any witnesses!"

"Or else when you think that no one can see you, like you did in the woods! I know!" countered Ricki.

"Well observed, Ricki! My compliments!" With these words he left the girl standing there and walked over to Carlotta.

"Did you all hear that? What nerve! That's unbelievable!" shouted Ricki heatedly, with both hands on her hips.

"Come on, don't get so upset. He's just trying to make you mad!" Kevin tried soothing her when they were together again.

"And he did a good job of it. What a jerk!" While Ricki was still fuming about Logan, Beth ducked under the paddock fence and went over to Rondo, who was dozing under a large apple tree.

"Oh, Rondo," she said, leaning against him. "I can't stand it anymore. They're all against him and I don't know what to believe and what not to believe. Can't you give me some advice?"

Rondo snorted softly and changed his weight to the other leg, hardly opening his eyes.

"I wish I had your peacefulness," sighed Beth and wrapped her arm around her horse's neck. Why did life have to be so hard?"

* * *

Carlotta and Logan disappeared into the house together.

"It looks like the moment of truth has come for Logan, after all," Lillian said pensively as she watched them leave. "Carlotta made a remark yesterday that she wanted the whole thing to be cleared up once and for all."

132

"Does that mean she's finally convinced that Logan is behind everything?" asked Ricki, interested.

"I don't know. She didn't say anything else, but if she's asked him to come into her office, there must be a reason."

"I would give anything to be a fly on the wall. I can't imagine what lies he's going to tell her."

Kevin looked at his girlfriend for a long time.

"You really hate him, don't you?"

Ricki nodded vigorously.

"You bet!"

"And how would you react if it came out that he's actually innocent?" Kevin pressed on. Ricki just waved him aside.

"I don't think I need to worry about that," she replied. "He's probably done more things than we even know about."

"You're so hard, you know that?"

"Only sometimes," answered Ricki.

"Hmmm ... and sometimes it really shocks me." Kevin began to wonder if he really knew his girlfriend as well as he thought he did.

"Oh, come on, I'm not that bad." Ricki tried to smile, but when she saw the serious look in Kevin's eyes, she couldn't quite manage one.

Inwardly, she was very upset.

"You – you don't really think I'm like that?" she asked softly. "Aren't there people whom you don't like right from the start, even before you really get to know them?"

Kevin nodded.

"Yeah, but you can't believe the worst of these people, just because you don't know them."

133

Ricki was silent.

What could she say? Ever since Logan had appeared on the scene, Kevin had been completely taken in by him. She was certain that the only way her boyfriend was ever going to see her side was if Logan's guilt was finally proven. Until then, they were probably going to continue having fights about their new classmate.

Chapter 9

After half an hour, Logan left the ranch house with a grim expression on his face, and when Carlotta followed him out shortly after, her look was unreadable.

"Well? Did she finish you off?" asked Lena, as he walked quickly past her.

"Yeah!" the boy barked back. "She's actually blaming me for everything. She only waited this long because she hoped I would come to her. Yeah, right! Like what was she thinking?"

Lena looked at him. "But I said that it was Cathy!"

"I don't care! At any rate, it wasn't me!" And with that, he stomped off toward his bike.

* * *

Hal was still deep in conversation with Cathy when his cell phone rang. Automatically, he answered with his usual, "Hi, it's Hal," but afterward, his expression changed to one of bewilderment.

"What? ... Why? ... Yeah! I got it! ... Okay! Bye."

Cathy hadn't really been listening. Lost in her own thoughts, she looked over to him, as Hal pocketed his cell phone and turned back to her, smiling.

"That's weird," said Hal.

"What's up?" asked Cathy, suddenly curious, and the boy took her aside.

"Listen up!" he said secretively, and then began to tell her.

* * *

"Carlotta, could I please make a quick phone call?" Cathy came running up to her, breathless. "I totally forgot that I have a dentist appointment. I really messed up and I'll never make it to the dentist's office in time, even if Rashid changes gears to turbo. Could I please call and cancel?"

Carlotta nodded. "Of course. You can use the phone in my office."

"Thanks!" she called, and went inside.

Lena watched Cathy suspiciously, and then she looked around. When she saw that no one seemed to be paying attention to her, she ran after the girl she hated so much, and slipped into Carlotta's house, making sure that the older woman hadn't noticed her.

As Cathy sat on the corner of Carlotta's desk, with her back to the door, talking to the dentist's friendly receptionist, Lena cautiously peered in. After she was sure that Cathy's conversation was going to take a while, she retreated hastily and glanced around the hallway. Her eyes settled on the small bureau where Carlotta always put all kinds of things. As usual, the car keys and registration papers were there, and today even her wallet lay on the top.

Lena hesitated for only half a second, then grabbed the wallet and opened it.

What a senile old lady, she thought. *How can anyone be stupid enough to leave all this stuff lying out in the open?* In a flash, she pulled Carlotta's credit card out of the slit and then put the wallet back where it was. Then she slipped silently past the open office door, to the connecting door leading to the stalls. Her heart was beating wildly at first, but when she finally stood in the stable without having been seen by anyone, she was able to breathe calmly once again.

Lena squeezed the credit card in her jeans pocket.

This thing is going to break Cathy's back! she thought, enjoying her plan immensely. Then she quickly entered the tack room. Frantically she looked all around. *Where did that horrid girl put her fanny pack?*

Lena searched the little room systematically until she finally found it near Rashid's saddle.

Instantly she grabbed it and tried to get the zipper open, but one of the teeth was broken and the zipper stuck.

"Darn it!" She hesitated when she heard Ricki's voice. Then with all her strength she tore at the zipper. At last the blasted thing opened and Lena stuffed the credit card inside. She had just enough time to put the fanny pack back where she found it and to pull a snaffle from the hook as Ricki and Lillian appeared in the doorway.

"Hey, what are you doing here? Are you going riding?" Lillian pointed to Jam's headpiece.

"Uh, no, I wasn't planning to. This thing fell down and I just wanted to hang it back up."

"Aha ... that 'thing' must be really heavy ... your face is

bright red from all the effort," joked Ricki, and Lena could have strangled her.

Quickly, she got rid of the snaffle and ran past the two girls. Outside, she almost ran into Cathy, who was about to enter the stable.

"Watch it, will you!" Lena yelled before running around the corner of the stable. From there, she saw Ricki and Lillian leave together shortly after. Cathy left a little while later.

Great! Lena congratulated herself. *That couldn't have gone better!* Then she ran off to look for Carlotta. She had some news for her.

Kevin and Hal had fetched Diablo, Sharazan, Rashid, and Holli from the paddock in the meantime, and were leading them toward the stable.

"Hey, it's time for us to ride back!" Kevin called to the girls.

While the four friends brushed their horses and saddled them, Carlotta listened attentively to what Lena told her. Then she opened her wallet and found that the credit card was missing.

"It looks like you're right, Lena. Come with me. We're going to get to the bottom of this right now!" Carlotta limped to the stable as fast as her bad leg allowed, with Lena following behind, the trace of a smug grin beginning to show.

Bev, who had just arrived at the ranch and was in the stable grooming Arabella, looked at her girlfriend curiously.

"Watch this!" Lena whispered conspiratorially. "In a few minutes you're going to see Cathy get thrown off the ranch."

* * *

"You want to ride home?" asked Carlotta, seeing the horses already saddled and awaiting their riders in the corridor.

Lillian nodded.

"Yeah, it's already late. We don't want Jake to have a fit again. You know him. He always gets upset when we're not home to get the horses fed on time."

Carlotta nodded, and then she looked at Cathy.

"Cathy, bring me your bag, please."

"My bag?" she asked bewildered.

"Your fanny pack."

"Uh ... Carlotta ... I don't have it with me, today."

"No?"

"No."

The ranch owner turned her gaze to Lena, who was perplexed for a moment, and then ran back to the tack room.

"Just a minute! ... Here! Here's the bag!" Triumphant, she swung it over her head.

"That isn't mine," said Cathy calmly, and turned to check Rashid's girth.

"But I saw you –" began Lena, as her friend Bev came toward her.

"Lena, that's *my* fanny pack. I just bought it yesterday and then I forgot I left it in the tack room."

"It's yours?" she stared at Bev, dumbstruck. "But I –"

"Nevertheless, I'd like to look inside," Carlotta reached out her hand for the bag, but Lena quickly hid it behind her back.

"I ... uh ... I think then, that I was wrong. Or ... " she began to stutter, but Carlotta insisted on taking the fanny pack from her, and immediately after opening it she pulled out her credit card. Without a word she held it up.

Bev shrieked.

"How did *that* get in there? That doesn't belong to me." Lena tried to save what she could.

"That's Carlotta's. And Cathy put it in there!"

Before Cathy could defend herself, Logan pushed past Hal and approached Lena.

"No she didn't." And without taking his eyes off the girl, he held out his cell phone, which had a camera, to Carlotta. "It was Lena! I took her picture while she was doing it!"

"What did you do?" Lena turned beet red. "That's impossible! I didn't see –" Immediately her hand flew to her mouth.

Carlotta nodded slowly.

"You didn't see anyone, did you? And now you just betrayed yourself!" she said severely.

Lena swallowed hard.

"You planned all of these awful things yourself, because of your jealousy, in order to get me to ban Cathy from Mercy Ranch. Isn't that true? Of course, it was unfortunate that Logan was also under suspicion. That's why you had to do something today so that only Cathy would appear to be guilty!"

Knowing her cruel scheme was about to be uncovered, Lena pressed her hands over her ears, not wanting to hear the rest of what Carlotta had to say.

"You fell into our trap, Lena! After my long talk with Logan, we asked Cathy to pretend she had to use the phone. And just as we thought, you sneaked in after her and took my credit card. You know, we're not as stupid as you thought we were. To be honest, I've suspected you for a while. However, today you finally gave me the proof of your guilt. You took the envelopes, too, after Cathy had left them lying in the tack room. It was also you who slashed my tires. And as far as the credit card goes, that was the last straw, Lena!" Carlotta's anger was at the boiling point.

"Get off my property, and hurry up about it! Don't let me see you here ever, ever again! I'm going to call your parents. And now, OUT!" Carlotta pointed to the stable door with her outstretched index finger.

"Carlotta ... I ... "

"You lied to me and you cheated me. Get out! OUT! IMMEDIATELY!"

The kids had never seen Carlotta that furious before, and silently the young people stepped aside to make way for Lena, who slowly walked past them with knees trembling, her gaze straight ahead. She began to walk faster until she ran out of the stable as though she were being chased by a mad dog.

"I guess that's that," commented Logan simply and reached out his hand. "May I have my cell phone back?"

Carlotta handed it to him and then smiled at Cathy and Hal.

"Thanks to the three of you for your help! You'd be good actors," she said, winking.

"No problem. I'll think about it," answered Logan.

"Hey, Logan, can I see that cell phone photo?" asked Kevin. Logan grinned.

"What photo?"

"What?! Don't tell me you didn't even take Lena's picture?" For a second Kevin was completely confused, and then he laughed.

"Clever! So you really fooled her?"

Logan nodded, and then left the stable to ride his bike home. For the first time in a long while, he felt good inside. Knowing that he was free of all suspicion made him pedal enthusiastically. *Carlotta isn't so bad after all,* thought Logan.

Ricki and Beth watched Logan as he walked out, and although the former still wasn't sure what had just happened, the latter was bothered by a terribly bad conscience. How could she have thought that Logan was a thief? Without a word, she ran outside hoping to catch him before he left for home. But Logan was already gone.

"Tomorrow," she whispered after him. "I have to talk to you tomorrow, and I hope you can forgive me, Logan!"

* * *

"Ricki, I'd like to talk with you." Carlotta gestured to her to come closer, and then she put her hand on her shoulder and led her outside. Slowly they walked together toward the paddock, where Carlotta stopped and forced Ricki to look her in the eyes.

"I really messed up, didn't I?" the young girl asked softly.

"Yes and no. Ricki, dear, you allowed the opinions of others as well as your own experiences to shape your feelings about Logan, but you never stopped to ask any questions. Unfortunately, we can't rely on the feelings of others, nor can we always depend on what we see with our own eyes. Sometimes certain situations that appear to be one thing when you view them out of context can turn out completely differently when the facts are known. Remember the envelope you saw Logan opening and thought it was mine – the one that had the money in it? Well, it was a letter from Beth that he always carries with him."

Ricki cast her eyes down.

"And the incident in the woods, when you thought you saw Logan cruelly beating Star? The truth is the horse had bolted and fallen into a ditch and couldn't or didn't want to get up again. What would you have done in Logan's shoes? He used a hazelnut branch to force his horse to get up, although it upset him to do it. It wasn't exactly the best method, I have to admit, but it worked."

"Oh Carlotta, I didn't know that. I ... I just saw him beating his horse."

"How could you have known? But you could have given Logan the opportunity to explain the situation to you before labeling him an animal torturer," Carlotta looked at her sternly.

"By the way, I had a call from Nick Rizzo today. He wanted to tell me that the culprit who slashed his car tires and spray painted the stable walls has been arrested. I've already forgotten what his name is, but the important thing is that it wasn't Logan!"

Carlotta paused to let Ricki process the information.

The teen replayed the past few weeks in her mind, weeks in which she had criticized everything about Logan, weeks in which she had fought with her friends about Logan. Finally she had to admit to herself that all she had thought and said about him were completely untrue. She had been thoroughly wrong about him, yet had taken every opportunity to let him know that she thought he was guilty of everything, and now she was so ashamed.

"A human being is just a human being," Carlotta

resumed. "And human beings make mistakes. Some make big ones, some make small ones, but no one is so perfect that he is without mistakes. We all can learn from our mistakes, but, my dear, you can only profit from mistakes if you don't repeat them. Do you understand?"

Carlotta affectionately brushed a stray wisp if hair away from Ricki's sad face.

"Everyone has to have at least a second chance to prove to himself that he has learned something. Logan did a lot of foolish things in New York, but I'm almost certain he will never do them again. So don't keep reminding him of his past mistakes; instead, offer him your hand, and accompany him for a little part of the way into the future. Only those who believe in themselves will find their way. However, if others also believe in him, a stony path will become smoother ... And as for you, child, I hope you have learned something from all this, and in the future you won't be so quick to judge someone."

Ricki nodded forcefully.

"Oh, Carlotta, I feel so awful, and so stupid!"

Carlotta smiled.

"You don't have to feel that way, Ricki." She patted her shoulder. "But I do expect one thing of you – I want you to apologize to Logan!"

"Oh, yes, I will. I promise! And not just to Logan, but to the others as well! I really behaved like an idiot! ... Thanks, Carlotta. Thanks a lot – for everything!"

* * *

The next morning Ricki woke up relatively early, full of energy and with a wonderful sense of freedom.

She got up quickly, dressed, and went over to the stalls where Jake was already busy.

"Good morning! Did you sleep well?" she called out to him and, on her way past him gave him an enthusiastic kiss on the cheek.

"Hey, hey, hey ... you're kissing an old man? What's with you this morning?" Jake grinned, but he felt that something had changed with Ricki.

"Oh, I could give the whole world a hug today!" beamed Ricki and wrapped her arms around her horse's neck.

"Which you just did. Diablo is your world, isn't he?"

"That's true! ... Hey, Jake, why didn't you tell me that I was being a total idiot?" she asked, teasingly.

"I did, but when you ladies have your minds set, you don't believe what an old man says anyway!"

Ricki grinned.

"You've probably had a lot of experience with that, haven't you?"

Jake's eyes twinkled and a smiled formed on his lips.

"That's for sure! Come on, grab a pitchfork! As long as you're here, you might as well help."

"Aye, aye, Captain!" Ricki gave a salute and then brought the wheelbarrow over to him.

"I'm so glad today is Saturday. The others are coming around ten o'clock and then we're going to ride over to Carlotta's. But before that, I have to go downtown."

"You guys are at Mercy Ranch a lot. What do you do there all day? And what about your schoolwork? Do you even have time to study?"

"Oh, Jake! Don't you start with school, too! Mom's bad

145

enough. She asks me the same thing every day! But you know what? On Mercy Ranch we learn things for life that we can't learn at school."

Jake stopped what he was doing for a moment.

"Oh, yeah? What, for example?" he asked curiously.

"Well, if I know how to get the square root of 7,941 that doesn't really help me in real life. But if I learn how to deal with my friends, then that helps me for the rest of my life."

The old man nodded in admiration.

"That sounds good, Miss Sulai! But do you know the square root of 7,941?"

"Nope," said Ricki. "But can you tell me how much roses cost?"

"Roses?" asked Jake, bewildered. "What made you think of roses?"

"I just did, that's all!" Quickly, Ricki finished her work, jumped on her bike, and rode off like the wind. If she wanted to be back by 9:30, she would have to hurry.

* * *

When Lillian, Cathy, and Kevin arrived shortly before 10:00, Ricki wrapped her arms around her boyfriend and held out a long-stemmed red rose.

"Huh? Did I forget that it was my birthday today?" asked Kevin, perplexed.

Ricki smiled at him.

"No! I just wanted to apologize to you ... actually, to all of you!"

"What for?"

"For everything. I haven't exactly been queen of nice these past few weeks," said Ricki. Then she looked at

146

Cathy and Lillian. "I would have liked to give you each a rose, too, as an apology for my behavior, but unfortunately, my empty wallet ruined that plan."

Lillian laughed.

"Oh, I know how that is! No problem. Your good intentions are enough. It's great to see you're your old self again!" she responded, and Cathy hugged her friend in agreement.

"Thanks! Then let's get going. I think I haven't been this excited about riding to Mercy Ranch in a long time!" And just like that Ricki disappeared into Diablo's stall.

* * *

Beth was at the ranch early that morning, too. She didn't want to miss Logan's arrival since she wanted to talk with him before he rode off on Star.

Completely absorbed in her thoughts, she stood beside Rondo brushing his coat, as she thought over what she would say to Logan.

"I wonder whether he'll even listen to me," she spoke to her horse. "Or maybe he'll just leave me standing here."

"I don't think he'll do that," answered Carlotta, who had approached unnoticed.

Beth jumped nervously.

"Gosh, you scared me. Good morning, Carlotta."

"Hello, Beth. You want to talk with Logan?"

The girl nodded.

"Yeah, but I don't know how."

"Hmm, if you let your heart speak, you'll be fine," responded the wise older woman. "Just tell him what happened and how you feel now. I think he'll understand."

"Oh, as if it were that easy ... But I'm going to try!"

"Good morning, everyone." Hal joined them.

Carlotta was taken by surprise.

"What's going on today? Normally you guys don't get here until the afternoon."

"Cathy and company are coming this morning, too, and we thought we could help you."

Carlotta had to laugh.

"I can't wait. You'll probably flirt with Cathy all day, and Beth will flirt with Logan, if all goes well. Frankly, I don't know if four teenagers in love will be much help. But they might add to my gray hair, if things don't go the way they want them to."

"Oh, Carlotta, don't say that!" grinned Hal, who was so excited to see Cathy again.

"Hi, everyone." Logan came through the stable door and waved to Hal and Carlotta, who waved back. When he saw Beth with Rondo he hesitated a moment, but he didn't show any reaction. Quickly he went over to Star and greeted him very happily.

Beth's spirit was deflated and she seemed to have shrunk.

"Good luck!" whispered Carlotta to her, and before she left, she gestured to Hal, with a jerk of her head, that he should leave as well. After all, it would be easier for Beth to talk with Logan if no one else was around.

"Please, somebody help me," whispered the girl, before taking a deep breath and leaving her horse's stall. She walked over to Logan with heavy steps.

"Hey," she said softly, without looking directly at him.

"Hey," replied Logan, and then the two of them stood awkwardly silent.

"I wanted –" they both began simultaneously. Then they both laughed, which managed to break the ice.

"Let me speak first," begged Beth, and suddenly everything she had been keeping inside during the past days and weeks burst out of her: her feelings and her thoughts. And when she finally didn't know what else to say to Logan, she whispered, "I care about you so much and I should never have hurt you like that. Please, forgive me!"

Logan felt his heart beating as he looked at her, speechless.

* * *

"Hey Carlotta, is everything okay?" Kevin jumped down from Sharazan directly in front of the ranch owner.

"It is with me, and apparently it is with you, too, the way you're smiling!"

"What else can you do but smile, when someone gives you a beautiful rose so early in the morning?" he asked, laughing. He gazed tenderly at Ricki, who smiled at Carlotta.

"I'm really glad that everything is cleared up between you two."

"Is everything cleared up with us, too?" asked Hal softly, looking pleadingly at Cathy.

"I don't know," she answered truthfully.

"Do you ... do you want to go out with me again? Even though I was such a jerk and left you for Lena?" Hal was relieved that the question he had wanted to ask Cathy the day before was finally asked.

Cathy looked at him for a long time before answering.

"At the moment, I'm not completely sure," she said slowly, but then she remembered what Ricki had said Carlotta told her, about always giving a person a second chance.

"Oh," responded Hal dejectedly, lowering his head.

But Cathy hadn't finished her sentence.

" ...At the moment I'm not completely sure, but we could try to rebuild our relationship slowly and see if we can get back what we had before. I'd be happy if we can manage that."

Hal's face lit up, and spontaneously he wrapped his arms around Cathy and gave her forehead a kiss.

"I think we'll manage!"

"I don't mean to interrupt this lovely reunion," said Ricki, looking around, "but where's Logan? Has he come yet?"

Carlotta acknowledged that indeed he was there, "but right now is not a good time to talk with him, I think." She smiled. "Him or Beth."

Ricki grinned.

"They can flirt with each other later! I just want to apologize to him really quickly. Look, Carlotta, see what I brought him as a peace offering." She reached into her backpack and took out a new currycomb.

"I saw that his was pretty worn out, so I thought he'd like to have a new one."

"Hah, now I know where you money went!" laughed Lillian. "Those brushes are expensive."

"Well, it's the least I can do after all the things I said to him."

Carlotta nodded encouragingly at Ricki.

"That's a lovely present! I'm sure he'll like it. He's in the stable."

"Thanks!" Ricki pulled Diablo after her, and when she had almost reached the stable corridor and was about to shout a greeting, she saw Logan pull Beth toward him and whisper something to her.

"Oops," responded Ricki quietly and led Diablo off to the side. "I think I won't disturb the two of them after all! It looks like they made up, doesn't it, boy? Well, I hope that he accepts my apology later. What do you think?"

Diablo didn't answer but Ricki had interpreted the situation correctly.

"I missed you," Logan was saying to Beth, when Star stretched out his neck far over the edge of his stall and gave a wet snort right between them.

"Ick!" Beth burst out, and Logan wiped his face dry, and then both of them started laughing happily.

"That horse just doesn't have a sense of romance," he said apologetically, but Beth gently touched her finger to his lips and answered, "As long as his owner is romantic, I don't have a problem with that! I'm so glad to have you back! And I'm never going to let you go again!"